EXPLORING
KANSAS

EXPLORING KANSAS

Text and Photographs
MIL PENNER

SOUNDS OF KANSAS
Inman, Kansas

Exploring Kansas is dedicated to my lovely granddaughters, Alyssa Reimer Penner and Sofia Lee King. They are my inspiration and my joy. It is my hope that we may preserve the beauty, peace, and abundance we enjoy in Kansas for them and all the children of the world.

Copyright © 1996 by Sounds of Kansas.
All rights reserved. Printed in Kansas.
Published by Sounds of Kansas
972 Arapaho Road
Inman, Kansas 67546
316-585-2389

Library of Congress Number 96-68634

ISBN: 0-9615597-8-0

Cover photo: A dramatic stormy sky at sunset
near Ashland on K-160

Designed by John Hiebert
Edited by Mary Campbell
Printed by Mennonite Press, Inc.,
Newton, Kansas 67114

Contents

INVITATION TO EXPLORE 6

NEW EYES FOR KANSAS 8

EXPLORING HINTS 10

EXPLORING BENEFITS 12

EXPLORING KANSAS

Abilene 14

Ashland 16

Atchison 18

Buhler 20

Burlington 22

Caldwell 24

Cherryvale 26

Colby 28

Columbus 30

Concordia 32

Cottonwood Falls 34

Council Grove 36

Dighton 38

Dodge City 40

Doniphan County 42

Elk Falls 44

Elkhart 46

Ellsworth 48

Emporia 50

Fort Scott 52

Fredonia 54

Harper 56

Hiawatha 58

Hillsboro 60

Inman 62

Jefferson County 64

Kingman 66

Lincoln 68

Lindsborg 70

Linn County 72

Lyons/Rice County 74

McPherson 76

Marion 78

Maxwell Wildlife Refuge 80

Meade 82

Medicine Lodge 84

Morland 86

Nemaha County 88

Ness City 90

Newton 92

Peabody 94

Pittsburg 96

Pratt 98

Rawlins County 100

Stockton 102

WaKeeney 104

Wallace County 106

KANSAS SAMPLER FESTIVAL 108

KANSAS EXPLORERS CLUB ` 110

TRAVEL INFORMATION 112

INDEX 118

An Invitation

Consider this book a personal invitation to explore the wonderful state of Kansas. The offer extends to people of all ages and in all walks of life. Our earlier books—*Kansas Journeys* and the *Guide* series—featured the beauty and diversity of the Sunflower State, and judging from your warm response we know that many of you enjoy traveling here. This time I want you to go one step further: I invite you to *explore* Kansas!

Let me tell you what I mean. As an explorer you reach a new and deeper level of awareness. You see the story behind the story. You become intimate with your destination; you see and feel things you've never experienced before.

In this book, *Exploring Kansas*, I've gone ahead, plowed the first furrow, just to show you what is possible. I describe visits with exciting people—the tiger lady, the windmill man, Wolf River Bob, and ordinary citizens with wonderful stories. I tell about a new friend who took me on a jouncing jeep ride near Wildcat Canyon in search of Butterfield Overland Dispatch stagecoach tracks. I recall how in one-hundred-degree heat I vicariously experienced the lonely drama of the Santa Fe Trail in the Cimarron National Grasslands. I narrate with gusto my eating

Watching sky divers at the Kansas Sampler Festival

odyssey across Kansas, enjoying the cuisine, charisma, and camaraderie of hometown restaurants.

It was the adventure of a lifetime, nine months and almost thirty thousand miles of exploring the heart of rural Kansas. Once I caught on to the concept of digging below the surface, looking over the next hill, and courageously asking questions, I discovered reality. I found the authentic experiences and old-fashioned values that are missing in the glitz and clamor of the

fast lane and in media depictions of modern lifestyles.

Only because of time and space constraints do I limit this book to forty-seven rural Kansas communities. I don't mean to imply that these are the only delightful places to visit. Instead, I want to convey that *wherever* you go in Kansas you'll be rewarded with a rich experience... to demonstrate by example how much joy and value may be discovered throughout the state.

The tree-lined main streets and homey little diners of Norman Rockwell vintage are still there. Grandpa's farm, real cowboys, the old drugstores, soda fountains, blacksmith shops, hedgerows, and flower gardens still reward the diligent explorer, and kids still ride bicycles on tranquil streets and in country lanes.

It would be a mistake to suppose that rural Kansans are provincial folk not in tune with the times. Quite the contrary; rural people are very much aware of current issues and very deliberately make their own choices. They hold on to proven values with one hand and embrace new technologies and ideas with the other. In Moundridge, robot welders automate a factory; Caldwell is the headquarters for world-class wilderness photographer Charles Phillips; Logan's Dane G. Hansen Museum features Smithsonian Institution traveling exhibits; Burlington hosts the world's largest manufacturer of plush toys; farmers fly; dairy cows wear transponders; and Abilene is the home of the impressive Eisenhower Library and Museum.

Sadly, not everything in rural Kansas is rosy. Many small towns, family farms, and landmarks are disappearing. Serious and complex problems beset rural communities. Change is inevitable, the functions of small towns are in flux, but often we lose worthwhile principles, historical awareness, and precious resources because of short-term economic expediency or because the public is uninformed. As an explorer, don't close your eyes to the problems. View them with honesty and experience them with compassion to become better informed and more responsive.

People look for many things when they explore: adventure, romance, mystery, roots, values, knowledge, memories, and always pleasure in the process. I found all that and more, and you will also. Once more I invite you to become an explorer. See Kansas with new eyes, and you will love it.

Airplane spraying a milo field in the background

New Eyes for Kansas

Exploring Kansas for pleasure is an art. To paint a picture an artist faces a subject and a blank canvas. What finally appears on the canvas depends on the artist's depth of perception. Only an artist with a keen eye for the nuances of color, texture, and form may have the rewarding experience of translating the real beauty of his or her subject to the canvas.

So it is with an avid Kansas explorer; it is the perception that yields the joyful reward. Spanish explorer Francisco Vasquez de Coronado had eyes only for gold when he came through Kansas in 1541. Because of his limited vision, he failed to see the potential of the land and the rich Native American culture.

The myth that Kansas is flat and drab is widespread—and false. The turnpike illusion and false modesty on the part of many Kansans perpetuate the myth. Once you practice the art of "seeing Kansas with new eyes" you will agree with me that Kansas is the finest state in the union. Day trips, weekends, and even extended stays throughout the state will reward you in many ways. This book's purpose is to demonstrate the joys and rewards of such explorations.

Put on "new eyes" when you explore Kansas. Let go of preconceived ideas of empty space and turnpike boredom. The state's beauty, its secrets, and its history are often subtle, wrapped in a veil that yields to patient exploration. Kansas's charm is like a prairie rose at dawn glowing through iridescent dewdrops; you must be there at just the right moment to see the dazzling beauty.

Compare your eyes to a camera lens. It "sees" only what you direct it to see. So it is with new eyes. You need to direct them. To guide you, I suggest the eight elements of rural culture my daughter Marci and I have identified: history, geography, architecture, commerce, cuisine, customs, art, and people.

HISTORY: Every community has a history. It can be hidden in a name, a stone house, an old fence, an idle farm implement, or a local legend. Look at a butter churn and think of the children that turned the crank; imagine a family around a kitchen table, kerosene lamp in the middle, spreading homemade butter on thick slabs of mother's rye bread. That's history.

GEOGRAPHY: Geography includes all of nature's wonders: the land and its birds, animals, trees, flowers, and grasses.

Nostalgic, rusty remnants of an old hay wagon

See the diversity of Kansas's soils: black, red, stony, sandy, swampy, and desert dry. Identify birds by their voices, animals by their tracks, and seasons by their colors.

ARCHITECTURE: Architecture deals with structures built by people. It reveals a community's dreams, conception, successes and failures, and ethnicity. Building materials tell much about the land nearby; the styles of houses reflect prosperity or hardship as well as nationalities and historical eras.

COMMERCE: Evidence of commerce—what people do for their livelihood—merges with history and architecture. Riverfront warehouses recall steamboat days, faint traces of the Chisholm Trail evoke cowboys driving longhorn cattle, and giant grain elevators everywhere remind us that agriculture is number one in Kansas.

CUISINE: Then there is the most delightful of all rural culture elements, cuisine. Little hometown cafes, church suppers, festivals, home cooking, and special recipes are the way to recapture the culinary delights of unique cultures and bygone eras.

CUSTOMS: Distinctive traditions, festivals, and lifestyles can still be observed in rural Kansas: fireworks, Dala horses, the Czech Festival, horse-and-buggy transportation, and more.

ART: Art is an expression of the soul and it is found everywhere if your eyes are focused on it. The simple railroad spike monument at Mount Sunflower, the elaborate spires of a church, or the celebrated works of Birger Sandzen all represent the spirit of Kansans.

PEOPLE: The rural people of Kansas are full of fascinating stories about one-room-school days, dust storms, winter fun, farm animals, and more. The older people are like an old-fashioned water pump: you may have to prime them, but once you start pumping, tales of yesterday gush forth.

Go out into Kansas with your new eyes. Look at a Queen Anne house, note the distinctive style, in your mind's eye see a brawny young carpenter driving that last square nail, and imagine him carrying his glowing bride across the threshold a hundred years ago. See the dynamic energy of Kansas now: farmers in green fields, shopkeepers welcoming you, and bands marching earnestly down main streets. With your new eyes see the future: school buses on country roads, houses under construction (round nails are almost obsolete now), and always a dawn with its glorious colors and chorus of birds.

Every mile, every day the scene changes. Baltimore orioles arrive and chatter, bees buzz in fragrant wild-plum thickets, and butterflies awaken to the rising sun. Each season has its own signature, and each region outshines the other in splendor. Kansas beauty is subtle, but once recognized it is awesome. We cannot conceive true art or beauty without an appreciation of nature's protoypes—flowers, clouds, and landscapes.

Train your new eyes to zero in on details. A barn is a barn, right? Wrong! Artists fathom their subjects to capture their essence. So can you when perusing a barn. Who built it? Why? Building materials and styles vary with regions, from pine and cottonwood (did you know cottonwood dries hard as iron?) to stone, adobe, and cement block. There are bank barns, crib barns, New England barns, Dutch barns, and round barns. Why the color? Why this style of rain hood? Why square nails? Why the ornate scrollwork? Answer these questions and you'll find yourself intimately involved with the lives of the builders.

So it is with all the elements of rural culture—history, architecture, geography, art, commerce, cuisine, customs, and people. A closer look at Kansas with your new explorer eyes offers adventure, romance, wisdom, knowledge, mystery, and enormous pleasure. Yield to the artist within you—explore Kansas.

Exploring Hints

Explorers go out into the unknown craving the excitement of discovery. Nevertheless they carry with them as much information about their destinations as possible. Here's some information that might make *your* journeys more comfortable, productive, and memorable.

LOCAL CUSTOMS: You'll soon discover as you explore Kansas that local customs, distances, road conditions, and seasons may affect your travels. Customary hours when restaurants, gas stations, and local attractions are open vary considerably across the state. Often in the west you'll find food and fuel services limited on weekends (except in large towns and at harvest time). In some towns all businesses close on Sundays. In the east you may find museums, attractions, and even restaurants closed on Mondays. For your convenience, information telephone numbers are listed in the appendix for places mentioned in this book. Please call ahead so you won't be disappointed.

SECRETS: To find a town's secrets, get personal; get involved with the life of a community. The best way to put someone in a talking mood is to make his or her cash register jingle. A good idea is to take along a shopping list of items you need anyway. Buy some batteries, gasoline, a piece of pie, or a gift. You may pay a little extra, but so what? You made a new friend. Start a conversation by asking about a local landmark or event, but be sensitive about local issues—school boundaries, public land acquisition, and environmental concerns. Opinions on these issues vary dramatically. Get the pulse of a community by listening to the cafe conversation. Except during harvest you'll see pickups parked near the most charismatic local cafes at coffee time.

SPACE AND WEATHER: It's fun to follow country roads, gravel and plain dirt. Once you're alone on the prairies the open space you encounter may paradoxically seem to close in on you. Don't let the majestic vastness overwhelm you, but rather embrace the sky and the land, and with your new eyes see the glory of it all for the first time—the wind rippling through the grasses or wheat, the land that was the buffalo's home, and the storm clouds gathering miles away. Enjoy this country, even its harshness, but remember that rain and snow turn land and roads into hazards for the inexperienced or unprepared.

TOURISTS AND EXPLORERS: There is a difference between a tourist and an explorer. A tourist by definition is traveling for his or her own pleasure. There's nothing wrong with that, but to develop a rapport with a community you must go farther and become an explorer who realizes that we are all part of a global community. People quickly sense a thoughtful attitude and respond in kind.

COURTESY: While traffic laws, of course, are the same everywhere in Kansas, local protocol and your own good manners will dictate that you yield graciously to wide and slow farm machinery on country roads. Please realize that farmers and ranchers are at work while you're on vacation. Also please respect private property. Don't open gates unless you have permission, then be *sure* to close them immediately. In fact, just asking for permission to enter a pasture, follow a stream, or look at an old barn is often a way to gain a friend with a story to tell.

GAMES: Exciting and educational are the games you can play with children and friends as you travel over the wide open spaces of Kansas. Be creative. Make up "see first" contests, or have check-off lists of birds, flowers, animals, three-legged windmills, or hitching posts in town.

"Mommy, Mommy, that's a magpie flying over there. See the white patches on the wings? I saw it first, I get five points."

"Stop, John, I'm sure that's a a patch of prairie roses. Mark a 'first' down for me."

"Daddy, you can't fool me. I know where we are. I followed

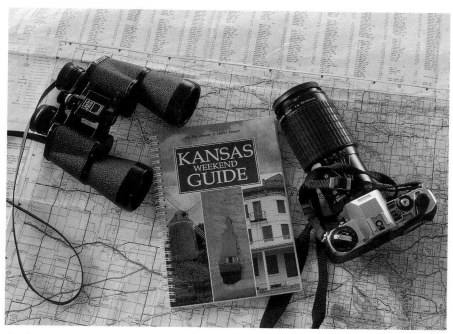

Basic Kansas Explorer's equipment

on the map; we're near Sun City."

GUIDEBOOKS: Books that identify flora, fauna, and geological features are readily available and will add to your pleasure. For an excellent free Kansas map call the Kansas Travel and Tourism Department at 1-800-2-KANSAS. Our book *Kansas Weekend Guide 2* gives directions to and phone numbers for more than fifteen hundred points of interest, attractions, and bed-and-breakfasts in Kansas.

PHOTOGRAPHY: Photography adds a wonderful dimension to any journey. Video recorders are great for capturing memories and the gratification of instant playback. A good still camera, however, actually helps you sharpen your new eyes. For this I prefer a camera with a manual focus, a zoom or a variety of lenses, and a tripod. As you focus and compose your picture your eye will become more discriminating. For example, you may see a street lined with blazing red maples. The first impulse is to snap a picture of the whole block. Then you notice one tree that's outstanding, one branch in particular. Finally you snap on a close-up lens, put the camera on a tripod, and zero in on one leaf. As you sharpen the focus, the dramatic colors, details of veins, and textures will pop out at you.

MOOD MUSIC: Heighten the spirit of adventure by playing stirring cassette tapes or CD's as you enter an unfamiliar community. Choose something that evokes an air of mystery and expectation. Michael Pickering, a Salina radio personality, offers the following suggestions: *The Ring* by Wagner; gospel music by the Statler Brothers; reggae by Bob Marley or Peter Tosh; "Battle Hymn of the Republic" sung by the Mormon Tabernacle Choir; or music by Mozart and Beethoven.

Editor Mary Campbell offered the following suggestions: The *Jupiter* Symphony, *Messiah*, Hungarian Rhapsody no. 12, Mannheim Steamroller's *Fresh Aire*, the *William Tell* overture, and Glenn Miller's "String of Pearls" and other big-band favorites.

RELAX: Let go of your adult cares as you explore. Foster a sense of wonder like that of a child. Allow yourself to go back in time as you climb the creaking steps of an old opera house; on a moonlit night near Castle Rock, listen for the spine-chilling call of a coyote; weep for a lonely, rustic village dying; taste the culinary delights of every region; and thrill to the sights of Kansas on the move—jet contrails tracing ribbons in the sky; black furrows chasing a plow; combines eating their way through golden fields; and the wonderful people of Kansas at work and play.

The Benefits of Exploring Kansas

Everyone in Kansas benefits when you travel in Kansas. You save money and enjoy yourself immensely, your dollars stay in Kansas, and your hosts appreciate your business.

Exploring Kansas offers many benefits besides the pleasure derived. Not only do you save a lot of your own hard-earned dollars and precious time, but your money helps drive the Kansas economy, especially in small communities. According to information compiled by the Kansas Department of Commerce and Housing, domestic and international travel expenditures in Kansas totaled over 2.5 billion dollars in 1993 (the latest statistics available); these expenditures generated 145 million dollars in state and local taxes. Leisure travel accounted for seventy-two percent of these figures. Kansans and other U.S. residents took 18.5 million pleasure trips (overnight or more than a hundred miles) within Kansas in 1994. Nationally, travel is the third-largest retail industry and is the nation's second-largest source of employment.

The point is that by traveling and enjoying ourselves in our home state we can make a significant economic impact. I'm not advocating isolationism, but I am suggesting that you examine leisure travel opportunities in Kansas as equal or superior to those in nearby states.

A tank of gas, a steak dinner, gifts and craft items, a book, or a night's lodging purchased in a small town make a difference. You'll enjoy the process of discovering Kansas crafters and artists—potters, quilters, woodworkers, painters, welders—entertainment, and local cuisine as you travel the state's highways and byways.

The economic health of many nonmetropolitan communities in Kansas is fragile. Some people say, "So what? Times change; small towns have served their purpose." Not so! Small communities are home to many people who love the place. The towns are a reservoir of values, history, memories, camaraderie, independence, and freedoms that are irreplaceable once lost. Consider also a town's infrastructure and the cost of replacing it in an urban area when the citizens must emigrate.

Rural Kansas is not all idyllic tranquility and unbroken contentment. There are hardships and poverty. Surveys and media reports relate crime in small towns, but the data usually include urban suburbs and bedroom communities.

There is unquestionably greater stability and harmony in parts of Kansas that are truly *rural*. I doubt the wisdom and humanity of a population shift

A large tour bus arriving in downtown Lindsborg

An artist's hands forming a stoneware vessel

quality time with children. July 4, 1804, becomes more than just a date in a history book when you see the spot where Lewis and Clark's band of explorers celebrated Independence Day. Geography and maps are exciting when children help plot a trek through the Flint Hills. Seeing a potter's wet hands squeezing squishy clay makes art look like fun, and a ride on Dolly the Trolley in Fort Scott is an unforgettable historical digest.

Informed citizens make a democracy work, and exploring Kansas illuminates many issues. All too often public policy is formed in response to a narrow sector of the population. The diversity of Kansas—economically, geographically, ethnically, socially, and vocationally—makes breadth of understanding essential. The inordinate influence of lobbyists and special interests can be tempered by an informed electorate... ordinary citizens who see the big picture. Just as one out-of-tune piano key affects harmony, so does one ailing element of our society affect the welfare of all. As you explore Kansas, you'll gain a more thorough understanding of issues vital to everyone's well-being.

Please, as you explore, see Kansas with new eyes; and feel its vitality as well as its anguish with your heart and soul.

toward metropolitan areas. With very few exceptions the residents of communities featured in this book say they feel secure and happy. Children are safe outdoors and it is considered an affront to lock a car on Main Street.

A surprising result of exploring rural Kansas for many people is that they fall in love with a particular place and end up living there. On numerous occa-sions I met transplants from California, Pennsylvania, Wisconsin, and other states, as well as former urbanites who had discovered rural Kansas and made it their home. They generally were surprised at native Kansans' reticence to praise their own state.

Another benefit of exploring Kansas is the education it imparts. It's a great way for parents and grandparents to spend

Abilene
City of the Plains

Abilene, City of the Plains, was named by Sylvia Hersey in 1857. She chose this beautiful biblical name even though she and husband Timothy lived in a dugout. Abilene's population had grown to about three hundred by 1867 when Joseph McCoy saw the potential of a stockyard where the Chisholm Trail intersected the approaching railroad. As Texas cowboys and their herds of longhorn cattle converged on Abilene, entrepreneurs, merchants, gamblers, and saloonkeepers rushed in to take advantage. The population swelled to three thousand and Marshal Wild Bill Hickock swaggered down Texas Street flaunting his deadly guns in a futile effort to keep the peace.

Exploring Abilene, I soon realized that I was retracing the steps of people with extraordinary vision—people like Sylvia Hersey, who saw beauty in what some called barren desert; Joseph McCoy, who in his imagination could connect millions of cattle running wild in Texas with a market in the East via a trail and iron rails; and a little Abilene boy who grew up to envision the Interstate Highway System.

You know, of course, that Dwight Eisenhower is a native of Abilene, but did you know that the late president was once spanked with a paddle at Lena's, an Abilene restaurant? Paddling people on their birthdays was a tradition at Lena's, and the tradition continues to this day in this charming country inn now known as Mr. K's Farmhouse Restaurant.

Architecture seems to bring out the sublime in visionaries. Certainly the mansion built by C. H. Lebold, an early Abilene banker, is more a statement than a matter of utility. The structure has twenty-three rooms with thirteen-foot ceilings, plus a basement, an intriguing attic, and a tower room above. But the sheer size impressed me less than the design, the stone work, and the interior decor. Incorporated into the basement and directly under the tower is the dugout home of Timothy and Sylvia Hersey. Even more amazing is the mansion's present owner.

Merle Vahsholtz and her husband, Fred, retired in 1975 from the farm machinery business. At that time the mansion was abandoned and deteriorating. The restoration took years of their own hard labor and the help of more than a hundred craftsman. Merle told me, "I had a dream to buy an old mansion when I was young. I collected period furniture all my life. . . . Everyone should have a dream. I enjoy giving tours, but I do insist on an appointment."

Other venerable Abilene structures open to visitors include the Seelye Mansion, the Kirby House, and the Tietjens Center for the Performing Arts. The Seelye Mansion, of Georgian design, was the home of A. B. Seelye, a distributor

The restored 1880 Lebold-Vahsholtz Mansion

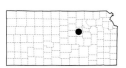

Statue of President Dwight D. Eisenhower

of patent medicines that could "cure" almost any ailment. There is no doubt that this highly alcoholic medicine was a smashing financial success when you visit the huge mansion its originator built in 1905. The house has twenty-five spacious rooms and a ballroom on the top floor. Nearby is a museum that displays vats and other apparatus used to process the "medicine."

I love exploring the Kirby House because it is rated as one of the best dining places in Kansas. My goal is to enjoy a meal in each of the eight dining rooms.

In an old church, now the Tietjens Center for the Performing Arts, the Great Plains Theater Festival presents live theater in Abilene. People who attended the old church for generations never realized that hidden above a false ceiling was a beautiful vaulted ceiling and that behind one wall there was a stage. The exterior resembles a medieval castle, an ideal setting for the *Passion of Dracula* advertised on the billboard when I was there.

What the Seelye Mansion, the Kirby House, and the Tietjens

Center have in common is Terry Tietjens, a man of vision who sees the future in the past. The incredible time and fortune that Tietjens has devoted to restoring these landmarks is a gift for the people of Abilene and its visitors to enjoy, reminiscent of a time when craftsmanship, lofty goals, and pride in one's work were virtues. By the way, Terry Tietjens gets up in the wee, wee hours of the morning to bake the fabulous breads and pastries served at the Kirby House. Asked how he could accomplish so much, Terry said simply, "You set goals."

A meditative walk through the Eisenhower Complex—the boyhood home, the museum, and the chapel where the Eisenhowers are buried—reinforced the thought that it's aspirations that divide the great from the mediocre. War hero and president, Eisenhower's great tribute to his hometown is Interstate 70 coming to Abilene.

Next to the impressive Eisenhower complex is a small metal building full of delightful and poignant surprises. Members of the Iowa Tribe from Kansas and

Nebraska have opened an American Indian Art Center headed by Patt Murphy. Paintings, pottery, bead work, and crafts produced by Native Americans are featured. Stop in for a look and some conversation.

Dickinson County's Heritage Center displays add to the visionary aspect of Abilene's history. In 1898 a young Abilene man built and operated the first local telephone exchange in the area. The company that Cleyson Brown founded went on to become the United Telephone Company. The Museum of Independent Telephony in the Heritage Center traces the evolution of the telephone industry in a very appealing display.

In a red barn nearby, a hand-carved C. W. Parker steam-powered carousel is featured and is available for rides on special occasions. The carousels were manufactured in Abilene at the turn of the century.

For more adventure take the Abilene and Smoky Valley excursion train, explore the Greyhound Hall of Fame, and enjoy shopping in a score of gift, specialty, and antique shops. For those with a sweet tooth the Russell Stover Factory Outlet means candy-making demonstrations and tasty samples. On top of all this, seventeen restaurants, six motels, and seven bed-and-breakfasts welcome you to Abilene.

Ashland

Airplanes, Buffaloes, and the Great Race

I have an impossible fantasy of flying an open-cockpit biplane, flying with the abandon of a nighthawk—soaring, hovering, diving—enjoying the moment.

It's a fantasy engendered in Ashland, Clark County, Kansas, where precision aerobatic aircraft, prairie wildflowers, roaming buffalo, and tricycles are important parts of a fascinating and eclectic exploration.

One of the prettiest airplanes I've ever seen, a red and white biplane, is sitting like a caged goose in the Pioneer-Krier Museum in Ashland. The plane, named the Krier Kraft, was built by Harold Krier, a legendary aerobatic flyer, who learned to fly at the Ashland airport. Krier competed in and won many national aerobatic events.

Tod and Jo Peterson, retired aerobatic pilots who operate the Ashland Airport, own two more Krier planes: a modified De Havilland Chipmunk, which may be seen at the museum, and the Great Lakes Special, built by Krier and his brother and hangared at the airport in flying condition.

The Ashland airport is one of few places in the country where aerobatic pilots may be trained. Low air traffic, an FAA-approved aerobatic box (air space reserved for aerobatics), and a grass runway make this location ideal. Jo Peterson says, "Grass runways are more forgiving than concrete runways, and they're wider." Visitors are welcome at the airport.

Other local men of note are featured in the Pioneer-Krier Museum: Wes Santee, 1952 Olympic gold medalist; Rodney Hardesty, world-acclaimed countertenor; and Jess Harper, early 1900s Notre Dame football coach. My eye caught an old Frazer car of about 1948 vintage. I courted V. Lee in a similar car, and I was taken aback to see it as a museum piece. On display in front of the museum is a nicely restored McCormick-Deering tractor. The restorer had put McCormick-Deering model W-30 decals on it. Farmer friends, let me know if you agree with me that it is a 15-30 model.

Enjoying nature from your car is feasible in many of Clark County's scenic areas. In fact, in the Big Basin buffalo have free range, and it's a good idea to stay within sight of your car. A few years ago, on a very windy late afternoon, I drove into the basin (it's a public area) to find St. Jacob's Well. It was an experience I'll never forget. I followed a stony up-and-down road with my little van far into the refuge, passing a herd of buffalo on the way. Finally I reached trail's end and a sign swinging madly in the wind that

An aerobatic airplane, Pioneer-Krier Museum

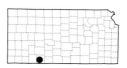

Free-ranging cattle on the road to Clark County Lake

said "St. Jacob's Well." A Bible verse spoke of Jesus resting at Jacob's Well in Samaria. Storm clouds were billowing in the east and lightning was playing in the clouds. The sun, low in the west, turned the clouds into the deepest, darkest blue I have ever seen. Stepping out of the van, I felt the wind rip viciously at my shirt.

Only a windmill gave relief to the horizon. I gauged the approaching storm and started down the steep path, slipping and sliding. The well is actually a small spring-fed pool surrounded by cottonwood trees. Even with the storm picking up, the pool's tranquility reached out to me. People say the pool has never gone dry; it is always there, waiting to give you peace.

A crack of thunder broke the spell. Climbing back to my van was no fun. Rain was pelting my windshield as I passed the buffalo stoically grazing in spite of the storm.

I came back to the Big Basin one morning last June. The buffalo were grazing in paradise, lush green grass sprinkled with gaillardia and a riot of colorful comrades. I noticed some yellow flowers I couldn't identify. (Later I called Phil Arnold in Ashland for help. He concluded that I had been puzzled by an Englemann's daisy, a pretty yellow flower, and bitterweed, an aromatic flower poisonous to livestock.) The flowers came right up to the edge of the roadway. Even a purple coneflower was a breathtaking sight imaged full frame with a close-up lens. At the other extreme, I suggest binoculars and a telephoto lens for the greatest enjoyment of the panoramic Big Basin vista from the road above it.

White limestone outcrops identify the Big Basin and the Clark County Lake as being in the High Plains, while sharp red bluffs and red soils place southern Clark County, including Ashland, Englewood, and Sitka, in the Red Hills. The Clark County Lake is in a rugged canyon, and, when viewed from above, white rocks and blue water contrast in a spectacular way. The fishing must be great; I always see fishing boats on the lake.

A fun way to see this beautiful country is to either enter or just watch Ashland's Great Race Memorial Day weekend. The first leg of the race is across the county lake by canoe, then an uphill runner takes the baton upslope where he or she hands off to a bicyclist. The race continues in open range country for twenty-four miles with runners, bicyclists, horse riders, and finally tricycles finishing down Main Street.

On the way to Englewood I realized that the only way to identify a creek in this dry country is to look for a bridge. The little town of Englewood (population 93) doesn't have much to offer any more, but the sign on the little Red Hills Diner is inviting: "Seating capacity 100, ten at a time."

Sitka, while still on the map, doesn't make it onto the population register, but you must stop in at the Old Weigh Station here for lunch or supper. It makes the West come alive.

May I suggest a day or two in Ashland for a pleasant, safe, relaxing interlude from life's stresses?

Atchison

Mystic River City

The Lewis and Clark expedition arrived by boat in the area of what would become Atchison, Kansas, on July 4, 1804. The expedition was exploring the Louisiana Territory, purchased from France in 1803. As a modern Kansas explorer traveling to the same place, I was humbled when I compared the ease of my car journey to the hardships of the 1804 adventure.

It was a midsummer evening, the last sunlight was beginning to fade, and a mist was rising from the river. On this hallowed spot, two couples casually drove golf balls across the river. As I turned north on the river drive, trees and darkness soon shrouded the river and engulfed either side of the narrowing, rocky road. I felt alone as I endeavored to relive an event that occurred almost two hundred years ago. I tried to imagine the primeval quiet that once must have lain upon the river, magnifying, by its stillness, the splash of a jumping fish or the stroke of an oar. Two motorcycles caught up with me and roared by.

I wondered whether the river's quiet strength still dominates the affairs of Atchison. Does the spirit live on of the mighty men who rowed and pulled a fifty-five-foot keelboat upstream to the continental divide?

My reverie was broken again as lights emerged once more out of the fog, erratically coming my way. Noisily they passed by, and I was very much alone; even the spirits of the river were gone.

Early the next morning I discovered evidence of another tenacious spirit. The Forest of Friendship south of Atchison is dedicated to Amelia Earhart, the pioneering aviatrix. The forest is a lovely concept. Trees from every state and thirty-five foreign countries rooted in common ground signify unity and friendship. An early-morning walk along the path of friendship is always inspirational. Look for Joyce Kilmer's poem engraved on the walk. Also imprinted on the walk are names of citizens—presidents, generals, entertainers, and many others—who pay tribute to Earhart's courage and inspiration.

Amelia Earhart, born in 1897, was the first woman to fly solo across the Atlantic Ocean. She died in 1937 in an attempt to fly around the world. The house where she was born is a stop on Atchison's historic structures walking/driving or trolley tours.

Atchison is old as Kansas towns go. It was established in 1854, seven years before Kansas became a state. Contrary to what I expected of a frontier town, it reflects an era of opulence and splendor rather than the bare bones of pioneer life. When the Kansas-Nebraska Act of 1854 opened the two frontier territories to settlement, entrepreneurs and speculators rushed to the scene. "Old money" families from the East arrived, investing fortunes in new enterprises and at the same time maintaining their lavish lifestyles.

The homes listed for Atchison's historic tours embrace this era. Many are private residences, but a number are open to the public. The Eva Cray home/museum welcomes visitors. This twenty-five-room mansion is furnished in Victorian style. Note the Scottish influence in the round tower, fanciful battlement, carved golden oak cabinet work, and curved-glass windows.

Statue of pioneer aviatrix Amelia Earhart

Atchison's Visitors' Information Center

Down the street the magnificent H. E. Muchnic home is now an art gallery open to visitors. My favorite mansion is the Drury Pennell house because they serve elegant luncheons and dinners. As I waited for lunch I thought about the grandeur these houses must have known: servants, fine clothes, social graces, power, and prestige. For some reason I wasn't envious.

Speaking of food, Paolucci's is a fine family-owned Italian restaurant on Third Street. This is a place where the family atmosphere and personal touch are palpable. Talk to the founder's grandson Ed Begley, now the manager; you'll soon see how proud he is of his heritage.

An elegant place out of town near Lancaster serves high tea at noon in the English tradition—salad, an antique crystal platter filled with English scones, breads and sweets, your choice of entree, a dessert, and English tea or coffee. Marci and I pampered ourselves there a few days before Christmas. I felt like a king, and the Christmas decorations were something to behold. Go! It's called the Haderway Tearoom. Ask for the story behind the name.

If you see a yoke of oxen pulling a wagon, you're probably close to Woolly Meadows, the home of Carol and Harold Spencer. Harold yokes up Big Bob and Little Bill every day when weather permits. On this family farm you'll find alpacas, wallaroos, a pot-bellied pig, macaws, and more. Call for information. Make a game of "who will see the first donkey [or goat, or whatever]" with your kids.

As I was hunting for Woolly Meadows I came upon an old, unpainted house with a sign saying "This Ol' House." Curious, I turned into the nearby farmyard. The farmer said to take the path to the old house. What can I say? June Friend had the house packed full of good stuff—homemade quilts, wall hangings, and antiques—another one of those rural surprises. Watch the dog, he's got a ten-foot chain.

Here is a suggested Atchison safari plan: Arrive the night before (good lodging in town), supper at Paolucci's, early-morning hike in the Forest of Friendship, stop at Santa Fe Depot visitor center (this is the Chamber of Commerce headquarters), and browse the Atchison County Historical Museum and the Atchison Rail Museum located here for area background. Board the trolley for a historic homes tour, lunch at the Drury Pennell House, stop at Cray House Museum and Muchnic Art Gallery, shop at Atchison Mall (first downtown mall in the U.S.A.). Take a relaxing river drive.

Plan the second day to see Woolly Meadows and This Ol'-House in the morning. Be sure to have High Tea at Haderway's.

Atchisonians are almost blasé about the Missouri River, allowing trees to screen it, but the steamboat era's entrepreneurial momentum is firmly imprinted on the town. Look for signs of it as you enjoy exploring Atchison.

Buhler
Dreams and Visions Realized

I remember Buhler well; it was the home of my grandmothers in the thirties and forties. Monday, washday, the day-after-church day, stands out in my mind. It was a point of honor to be the first to hang spotless white wash out on the line.

The maxim "cleanliness is next to godliness" still describes Buhler today. Vicki Adrian, a Los Angeles native, recalls her first glimpse of Buhler: "It was so clean and neat; that's the first thing I noticed."

The events we now call history were for my grandmothers merely the "goings-on" of people reaching out too far on a limb. When my grandparents (they were children at the time) and their friends arrived in the area in 1874, Buhler was a windswept prairie knoll. A monument on the hill where they gazed over the Blaze Fork valley marks the spot where one of the pioneers said, "This is a hopeful meadow view," and they named their congregation Hoffnungsau (hopeful meadow). Stop here and with your new explorer eyes see the farmsteads, wheat fields, and irrigated corn fields now in the valley as they must have been envisioned by these Mennonite pioneers.

To the north and east these Dutch/Prussian/Russian wanderers saw a gently rolling (almost too flat for good drainage) treeless plain covered with tall prairie grasses. They were quick to note the deep black soil, ideal for the Turkey Red wheat seeds stuffed in their steamer trunks. A mile south of their vantage point the Little Arkansas River bordered miles and miles of sand dunes—not the least bit attractive to these unbending farmers.

The Little Arkansas River near Buhler is a dramatic line of demarcation between the Wellington-McPherson Lowlands (black clay/loam soils) and the Arkansas River Lowlands (sedimentary sand). Topographic boundaries are seldom this well defined elsewhere in Kansas.

Given a little bright sunshine, the sand hills always seem warm and cozy on a winter day. No doubt the plum thickets and tall grasses cut the cold wind, but it's the warm colors and texture of the sand on the sunny side of a hill that quicken the soul. V.Lee and I often walk the trail in the Sand Hill State Park west of Buhler. I like to pretend I'm the first explorer to trek across these awesome dunes, I ponder the cataclysmic winds that shaped this land, and I think about all the animals and birds that once shared this lovely place with us. We climb the highest hill to find Buhler's white grain elevators rising above the dunes, with Moundridge, Hesston, Inman, and McPherson on the far horizon.

A first-of-January bird-watching safari to the sand hills between Buhler and Hutchinson was an annual affair when our kids were small. I remember one country road where thickets (including poison ivy) and a cottonwood canopy a mile long created a birder's paradise—chickadees feeding upside down, red cardinals framed in earth tones, yellow-shafted flickers flashing their bright trademark, quail running in their exaggerated posture, a congregation of sparrows, and slate-colored juncos in their little tuxedos.

Back in Grandma's day, Sam Schneider was a big name in Buhler. I recall hushed grown-up conversations about Sam's grandiose "goings-on." Maiden Aunt Lizzie said, "This is too much for someone from Buhler." In 1936 Schneider built a large filling station on Main Street that purportedly was the first super-service gasoline station in the nation. I vaguely remember a *Popular Mechanics* magazine photo touting a Sam Schneider semi-trailer tanker as the ultimate in fuel

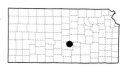

Wheat sculpture in Buhler's Wheatland Park

transportation. The Schneiders' distinctive house with its red-tile roof is still one of the finest in Buhler, and a large, diagonal-roofed "drive through" marks the super station, now housing a number of businesses.

The triumph of pioneer vision has awed many more generations of skeptical observers in Buhler. Consider these statistics for a town of thirteen hundred citizens: Buhler's schools, District 313, send out a fleet of forty-three buses to transport more than twenty-two hundred students; state-of-the-art Gregory Inc., printers of full-color computer-generated graphics, employs 120 workers; Cal-Maine Foods processes sixty thousand *dozen* eggs per day, many produced near Buhler; and that's just the beginning.

Phil Neufeldt, second-generation operator of Neufeldt Interiors, says, "Cleanliness, craftsmanship, integrity, all are virtues passed on to us from our Christian founders. Look at the businesses here on Main Street. You'll soon see that quality and service are important to all of us." Phil's attractive showroom is in the old Sam Schneider super station, integrating history and fashionable decor.

Indeed, a walk down Main Street bears out Neufeldt's statement. As you enter Bartel Cabinet Shop the stamp of craftsmanship is obvious. To provide space for their extensive woodworking and refinishing operation the Bartels converted an old mechanic shop and a filling station on the 200 block to very attractive offices, display rooms, and workshops. The building fronts reflect an early western motif, enhancing the Buhler charm.

Be prepared for a kaleidoscopic sensory barrage as you enter Adrian's A to Z Gifts and Furniture. Color and design attract the eye to an array of furniture, home accessories, framed prints, and lamps. Soft music and delicate fragrances invite you to browse among tempting jams and jellies and little creatures irresistibly touchable—Cherished Teddies, Precious Moments, Dreamsicles. Folks from all over Kansas love to visit and shop here.

Wheat has always been the economic base of the Buhler community. A large Archer, Daniels, and Midland flour mill and a Mid-Kansas Co-op elevator dominate the scene. Huge farm trucks wait in line here at harvest time to unload; it's a sight worth seeing. The first flour mill in Buhler was built in 1891. Nearby, the restored house (circa 1898) of John Wall, pioneer miller, represents early Mennonite culture.

Heartland Haus offers antiques, light refreshments, and delicious ice cream; Lavon's Bakery and Bar-BQ is the place for delicious luncheons and carryouts; and at Sandy's Kitchen you can get breakfast, coffee, lunch, and the talk of the town. For borscht, verenika, smoked German sausage, zwieback, cherry mos', and peppernuts you'll have to come to a church supper or wangle an invitation from one of the Mennonite families in town.

Don't leave Buhler without a stop at Wheatland Park, where graceful ripening heads of wheat, sculpted in metal by Milo Schroeder, metaphorically connect life springing from the earth to lofty aspirations. It's a fitting symbol of how pioneer hopes and dreams have been realized in this thriving prairie town.

Burlington
The Friendly Little Red Caboose

The little red caboose is the place to go in Burlington. Right in the heart of town, at the intersection of U.S. 75 and Neosho Street, Diana Gunlock, the Coffey County Chamber of Commerce director, warmly welcomes Kansas explorers. She points out places of interest, and offers helpful information. Adjacent to the chamber office is a large parking area and spacious, clean rest rooms for the traveler's convenience (nice for bus tours).

On East Neosho, following Diana's directions, I found a veritable menagerie: gorillas, elephants, raccoons, skunks, and the cutest teddy bears I've ever seen. I watched Bud Strawder take a baby pig out of a box. The little pig seemed hungry, so Bud fed it from a bottle. The way it lunged for the bottle and grabbed with its little feet perplexed me for a moment.

I was in the Country Critters Puppets and Plush Toys showroom. It's a treat for kids of all ages to see these lovable puppets, plush toys, and ride-on toys manufactured in a Burlington plant covering almost an entire city block. The showroom is open Monday through Friday, and factory tours may be arranged. I was fascinated by the manufacturing process; huge presses cut material, sewing machines and fans whir as about fifty skilled local workers create these cuddly lifelike creatures. Country Critters is the largest manufacturer of plush toys in the world.

Walking back downtown I couldn't resist peeking into some of the neat shops on Neosho Street. Small-town pharmacies are almost always interesting, so I went into Johnson's Family Pharmacy and was instantly drawn to the old soda fountain. I ordered a cherry phosphate; sure enough, they had the makings for it. I'm not sure whether it's always done this way, but the waitress measured out the phosphate with an eye dropper. I think it was about five drops—must be powerful stuff.

Personally I've never bought any quilting supplies or patterns, but I like to go into fabric shops just to absorb the color. If color is a criterion for fabric shops, Silver Threads and Golden Needles rates "fantastic." Merry's Crossing is also full of exuberant colors. Diane Merry's radiant shop has two rooms, one a flower shop and the other a full-line gift shop.

Across the street I met Brandon Hargreaves, who was just putting the finishing touches on his new Longhorn Steakhouse and Saloon. Given his youthful enthusiasm, the steaks will surely be succulent and the atmosphere congenial.

The public buildings in Burlington are impressive. The elementary school landscape design would flatter most university campuses. The middle school, the high school, the USD 244 Recreation Center (six-lane swimming, racquetball, dance room, indoor jogging track, and more), the library, the hospital and retirement village, and the airport were all either built or extensively remodeled in the last twenty years.

At the new library a life-size bronze sculpture, called "Sharing," depicts a grandmother reading a book with a little boy who's in baseball attire. It's a heartwarming reminder that the joy of reading isn't all in words.

The Coffey County Historical Society's Museum, another recent addition, is an example of modern architecture designed to blend into the small-town environs. The museum's spacious, well-lit displays include a bright red Mack fire truck, gleaming brass radiator Ford Model T, 30s-vintage country school stage curtains, a

Burlington's Main Street Visitor Center

collection of 140 dolls, and a model railroad layout.

The Wolf Creek Nuclear Generating Plant is a boon to the county's economy, both as an employer and as a source of tax revenue. Tours of the plant are available with 30-day advance reservations. The Wolf Creek Environmental Education Area offers the public three wildlife trails. A brochure interprets the trail's numbered signs. The South Pond Trail and the Prairie Lake Trail are each one-half mile long and are asphalted to accommodate wheelchairs. The Kansas Nature trail winds through a natural setting for 1.6 miles on a mowed-grass walkway. There's a bird viewing blind next to the cooling lake.

For nature lovers the John Redmond Reservoir and the adja-cent state and national wildlife areas present birding, fishing, hunting, and water recreation pleasures. Bald eagles may be seen during the winter months. Coffey County has often been referred to as the state's catfish capital, and lunkers weighing nearly a hundred pounds have been reeled in. For sightseeing, the rolling hills of the Neosho Valley offer a wonderful variety of grasses—big bluestem, little bluestem, Indian grass, switch grass, and sideoats grama—and wooded areas of elm, black walnut, hickory, ash, hackberry, cottonwood, and cedar.

A remnant of yesteryear lingers near the Neosho River on the extreme east end of Kennebec Street. The old Excelsior Mill, now only a limestone shell, stands there lonely, wait-ing for someone to restore it, perhaps as a factory or restaurant. Glowing in the late afternoon sunlight, the stones radiate a warmth that steel and concrete cannot equal.

Beto Junction, north of Burlington on U.S. 75, is not recognized as a town, but it definitely is an institution. In the late 1800s the name Beto was coined to designate the intersection of roads leading to four cities: B for Burlington, E for Emporia, T for Topeka, and O for Ottawa. It's said that Beto Junction has had four locations in the last hundred years. When the Roe family built a truck stop at the junction of I-35 and U.S. 75 they named it for the lost roving town. Of course, I've been to truck stops before, but this time as a Kansas explorer, I entered with anticipation and new awareness.

The sight of rows and rows of eighteen-wheelers, with their massive front ends, an abundance of chrome, many colors, and such diverse shapes and cargoes is stirring. Inside, the kings of the road have their own dining area, telephones within easy reach. It's a different world: friendly, lively with the camaraderie of strangers passing on the road. The public is most welcome at the restaurant, gift shop, and gas pumps. Check it out.

Burlington and Coffey County are eager to visit with you. See them soon.

Caldwell
Ghost Riders of the Chisholm Trail

There's a lot of exploring to do in Caldwell, and it may be up to you to do it. For one thing, I hear rumors of three Caldwells existing at the same time. How can this be? The state map shows only one Caldwell, with a population of fourteen hundred....

An air of mystery pervades Caldwell, alias the Border Queen. I suspect the mystery has to do, as happened to Ebenezer Scrooge, with the past haunting the present and future. One even hears of talking tombstones.

Indeed, an apparition—the Ghost Riders of the Chisholm Trail—greets you as you enter Kansas south of Caldwell on U.S. 81. Seen through the new eyes of a true Kansas explorer, these life-size steel silhouettes of cowboys, longhorn steers, and a chuck wagon call forth spirits of Caldwell's Border Queen days. This giant tableau, set on a red bluff in a pasture, commemorates the time when thousands and thousands of longhorn cattle and their attendant cowboys passed through on the Chisholm Trail.

Paradoxes abound in Caldwell. The present seems almost mundane as echoes and shadows from the past still clamor for attention. Homes in town are modest and the people work hard. Farmers and ranchers come into town in pickups spattered with red mud, and the ubiquitous Co-op elevator looms nearby. Wheat is king here; it almost seems as if the town waits in repose for the wheat to ripen. Yet the Border Queen still loves to flaunt its tumultuous glory days. Brass markers and brassy citizens blatantly tell the story, with tales of Henry Brown (a bank-robbing marshal), eighteen saloons and fourteen brothels, and escape tunnels leading out of gambling rooms in hotels.

While excellent markers detail and identify fifteen dramatic points of interest, it takes careful exploration to find the bullet holes in an old opera house, Boot Hill in a wheat field, and a cracked sidewalk that betrays a gambler's tunnel. Some off-the-record voices go so far as to say slot machines are still waiting under the streets to be fed silver dollars.

Jesse Chisholm's trail and the cattle drives were very real and important factors in the development of Kansas, and evidence of them can still be seen by those who are willing to look for a subtle swale in unbroken pasture or a railroad embankment stopping at the Oklahoma line. The fact that Caldwell is located two-and-a-half miles north of the Oklahoma line

Mural depicting elements of Caldwell history

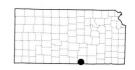

harkens back to the Cherokee Strip. A surveyor's error misplaced the Kansas-Oklahoma border for a time.

Sometimes confused with the Cherokee Strip is the Cherokee Outlet. This 58-by-226-mile tract just south of the Kansas border was given to the Cherokee tribe in 1828 by the United States government in exchange for other lands. In the late 1800s promises to the Cherokee were forgotten as land values increased. At noon on September 16, 1893, a gunshot started one of history's greatest races as a hundred thousand would-be-settlers raced to stake forty-two thousand claims in the Cherokee Outlet.

Still very real in present-day Caldwell are some of the places identified by the brass markers as historical. The Stock Exchange Bank, built in 1881, has a new front facade, but inside the atmosphere proudly speaks of the formative years—pictures of cowboys meeting in those very rooms and cattle horns with a span of seven feet, two inches.

Many of Caldwell's Main Street buildings witnessed the excitement of the Cherokee Outlet more than a hundred years ago. I touched the stained stones of the Cherokee Strip Center and walked into the Last Chance Bar and Grill. As I gazed out of a window, the cars and trucks I saw in the street became horses, wag-

Gunfighter's bullet hole in opera house wall

ons, and buggies poised for the great race.

Publisher Damon Weber writes, "New Mexico? Arizona? Paris? No, Caldwell may well be the fastest-growing art center." In three of Caldwell's venerable Main Street buildings you'll find the studio, offices, and workshop of world-class wilderness photographer Charles Phillips. Phillips studied the craft of black-and-white fine art photography under Ansel Adams in the 1970s but has evolved his own unique style. By using highly sophisticated photo enlarging and printing techniques, Phillips's photographs retain detail and tone beyond what the human eye could see at the original scene.

On the other side of Main Street in the Eddie Morrison Studio and Gallery, Caldwell presents the Native American three-dimensional art and jewelry of Eddie Morrison and the fiber loom artistry of Anna Petrik. Other Caldwell artists include Brenda Lebeda Almond, whose delightful pioneer mural overlooks the Heritage Park on Main Street; Mary Lou Ryland;

and Frances Kloefkorn.

My second morning in Caldwell, quite confused by Caldwell's nebulous identity, I had my toast and coffee in the Corner Cafe. The best in the West it was not, but the day's price of wheat was posted on the wall and every table was occupied with happy customers wearing baseball caps. My bill was only fifty-three cents, another Caldwell time warp.

I was enjoying myself immensely in Caldwell, reliving the cowtown excitement; visiting the Phillips Studio and seeing the wonderful wilderness prints and the huge enlarger used in the process; meeting sculptor Eddie Morrison, a Cherokee Indian, and candidly discussing the Cherokee Strip celebrations; riding out to the Chisholm Trail sites with Dave Williams as he told me stories of the era; and discovering more fascinating information at the Border Queen and Cherokee Strip Museums.

Karen Sturm put all this business of past, present, and future together for me at coffee in the Harvest Home Cafe (two coffees and rolls for $1.60). She conducts the "talking tombstone" event at the cemetery.

"We've come to the conclusion that our heritage—the glamour, values, and roots—is our future," she said, with pride and reverence for Caldwell's colorful legacy.

Cherryvale
Spring Is Coming

Cherryvale—what a romantic name. Can't you just picture a grove of blooming cherry trees in the heart of town? Imagine the fragrance of thousands of blossoms floating down Main Street. Maybe Camelot will come to Cherryvale some day, but for now the blossoms are only a dream.

Three things stand out when you explore Cherryvale: the restored Santa Fe Depot, Big Hill Lake, and the Bender Murder Mystery. I've been to Cherryvale three times and have discovered that my impression of the city is colored by whichever focal point grabs my attention first.

The first time I entered Cherryvale was on a swinging and swaying excursion train whistling its way from Coffeyville to Cherryvale. The train's passengers were tour-bus operators and travel writers invited to a familiarization tour of Southeast Kansas. The bleak, rain-drenched countryside was anything but inspiring, and the forlorn trackside backyard entry into Cherryvale didn't improve matters.

Like a rainbow on a bleak day, the Santa Fe depot elevated our expectations. Enhanced by the rain, the red bricks and red tile roof sparkled with renewed luster. With two carloads of people disembarking, people there to greet us, and the station freshly restored, it was easy to picture the activity as a daily event.

Inside, the building was equally impressive as citizens offered tea and coffee and extolled the virtues of Cherryvale.

We were told that in 1899 twenty-eight passenger trains a day entered Cherryvale. A photograph dated early 1900 showed a locomotive, black smoke towering amid bustling activity, right beside the depot I was in. Indeed, Cherryvale claims to have had the largest zinc smelter in the world because of its railroad service, its proximity to the mines, and what they once thought was an inexhaustible supply of natural gas.

In the town's heyday, Cherryvale bricks were touted as the best in the world. Again it was the confluence of natural resources—unique shale and natural gas—with the railroads that spawned the industry. The famous "don't spit on the bricks" bricks were produced here. A doctor in Topeka started a pioneer sanitation campaign using brick slogans, including, "swat that fly" and "bat that rat."

The Frisco Depot, built in 1900, has been razed. All the bricks and boards were numbered, crated, and for some reason stored in Springfield, Missouri. The industrial-boom years are reflected today in block after block of aging but serviceable brick streets and modest homes built originally for blue-collar workers.

Restored Santa Fe Depot in Cherryvale

Infamous Bender's Mound northeast of Cherryvale

Elsewhere in my Cherryvale memories I see shaded, meandering roads; fishing boats in calm coves; and people playing in delightfully clear, cool water and on sandy beaches. Campers love Big Hill Lake for its many shaded campsites (148 in all, most with electrical hookups). A unique one-mile walking trail passes through wooded hills referred to as the Little Ozarks. Red oak, post oak, chinquapin oak, and black jack oak abound here, providing acorns for wildlife. There's also a seventeen-mile horse trail with three turfed parking areas and camping facilities.

It seems that Big Hill Lake was named for Big Hill Creek, which originates near Big Hill, which in turn was named for an Osage Indian chief the white settlers called Big Hill Joe. Early settlers' reports tell of Osage Indians living in the area as late as the 1870s. In an article preserved in the Cherryvale Museum, a Mr. George Cunningham states that six hundred Osage Indians were camped on his father's farm when he bought it. The same article mentions that Emanual Mortimer and son Tom noted many cherry trees growing and Indians camping in what is now the Cherryvale area in the spring of 1867.

Then there is the Bender story. How many unsuspecting travelers on that lonely trail (1871 to 1873) from Leavenworth to Coffeyville succumbed to the siren call of voluptuous Kate, and what happened to the Bender family (an alias for four unrelated felons) after their grisly secret was discovered? Did Kate and Ma charm the sheriff in Oswego into letting them go? The mystery remains.

Somewhere behind what is now called Bender Mound (visible from U.S. 160), the Bender family set up shop as a two-room inn. Guests were invited in and seated next to a canvas room divider. When they leaned back against the canvas—bam, bang—a hammer descended and a trap door in the floor finished the job. When neighbors finally got suspicious, eleven bodies with cracked skulls were discovered in shallow graves.

The intriguing story of the Benders can be followed in detail at the little Cherryvale Museum. By appointment, curator Fern Morrow Wood, author of *The Benders, Keepers of the Devil's Inn*, will tell you the rest of the story.

Conversation with Fern Wood and a visit to the museum are good ways to get in touch with the town's exciting past. For instance, there's another mystery that remains unsolved. A white gravestone of a Spanish American War veteran stands in the Fairview Cemetery with only the name, vital dates, and military status on the stone. Yet the life of Cherryvale's Frank E. Bellamy may have touched us all.

The nation's Pledge of Allegiance is attributed to one Francis "Frank" Bellamy. The story is complex, but Frank told a friend that he had written the original text as an entry in a contest sponsored by the *Youth's Companion* magazine in the late 1800s. Frank received twenty-five dollars as a prize. A magazine office employee, another Francis Bellamy, later claimed that *he* wrote the pledge.

Not a glamorous tourist town, Cherryvale, however, is a gold mine for explorers, full of mystery and fascinating nuggets of history. Your new explorer eyes are necessary here to see the cherry blossoms, past and future. Cherryvale needs your support, and you need Cherryvale to see Kansas honestly... and perhaps to see "one nation, under God, indivisible, with liberty and justice for all."

Colby

The Oasis on the Plains

Colby, Kansas—to my surprise it felt like coming home, as much to a time as to a place. This is not to say that Colby is an anachronism; Colby is very much in step with the world. It has a progressive community college, its cultural facilities are up to date, and it has a full-service business district. It's also right on Interstate 70, where you'll find contemporary food and lodging plus a large factory-direct outlet center offering apparel, gifts, and cookware. Colby is a beautiful community anyone would be proud to call home.

Colby also wisely treasures the values and roots that made the community what it is today. I grew up on a McPherson County farm in the 1930s never realizing that I was living in the worst of times; the Depression, the drought, hard work, frugal living, and unswerving faith in God and country were the norms. The Colby Prairie Museum of Art and History tells a similar story of rural life in the early 1900s in a powerful way. The museum not only lifts out vignettes of family farm life, it also speaks for the value of the family farm in our country.

The Prairie Museum focuses on two quite different aspects of culture: the Kuska Collection of fine glass, ceramics, dolls, clothing, textiles, and furniture; and a Prairie Living display that includes the largest barn in Kansas. At first it seemed to me that treasures of the kings and early-twentieth-century rural life made a peculiar mix. The truth of the matter, however, is that prairie citizens, even though people of the earth, always aspire to finer things, as did the Kuskas, who lived in Colby for forty years.

The process used to make some Meissen ware, a unique hard-paste porcelain, was so valuable to a European king that in 1709 he imprisoned its inventor to protect the concept. One outstanding Meissen piece on display here, "the Good Life," represents the court of Louis XV. Among a collection of two thousand prized dolls is "Rocharde," a French fashion doll wearing an elegant gown, a genuine ermine cape, and a necklace showing, when magnified, famous paintings hanging in the Louvre in Paris.

I was a boy once more as I stepped into the parlor (always reserved for company) of the Eller House, a modest 1930s farm home. There were plush chairs like Grandma had, a little table with a *Needlecraft* magazine and *McCall's Pattern News* on it, and a large, dark piano with heavy turned legs. Out of context in the parlor (in my experience) was a black radio with a row of mysterious knobs. Push-button light switches centered in a brass plate, a carpet on the floor, and a vivid landscape scene on the stovepipe opening cover filled out my memories.

The reverie continued in the other rooms. I'll never forget how the mystery of the oil-burning Servel refrigerator intrigued everybody at our house. The Monarch cookstove in the Eller house was much like ours too, except our fire-starting box was filled with shingles instead of corn cobs. The crank telephone on the wall brought up an

The Spirit of the Prairie, Thomas County Courthouse

image of Pop asking, "Line 12 busy?" before he cranked the phone (there were seventeen families on our line).

Down the walk a bit from the Eller house, the Nicol one-room schoolhouse, District 15, evoked another round of memories: Millet's *The Angelus* and pictures of George Washington and Abraham Lincoln on the wall; recitation benches in the front; desks with inkwells; and little lunch pails on a bench. The brass handbell reminded me of school discipline—when it rang we were instantly attentive.

A sod house, Colby Prairie Museum

Fine and wonderful as everything else at the museum was, it was the huge Cooper Barn that completely enraptured me. Just its physical dimensions are astounding: 114 feet long, 66 feet wide, and 48 feet tall. Originally built in 1936 for Foster Farms near Rexford to house seventy-five head of show cattle, the barn was moved to Colby in 1991. It is in mint condition, its hayloft and its carrier track, bins, and pens intact. The Colby community enjoys many barn dances in the hayloft.

It is the exhibit in the barn that ties all the elements of the Colby community together, and perhaps of western Kansas and the High Plains as well. *Prairie Grasses to Golden Grains: Agriculture in Northwest Kansas 1870s to 1990s* forthrightly begins with the land itself, describes the

Native American period, and moves on through sometimes surprising issues to the present. This great work begins in one corner of the barn and moves around the circumference and through the middle. Easily readable informative plaques and original photographs accompany well-chosen artifacts to tell the story.

For example, the early-pioneer-period display includes a horse-drawn sodcutter that sliced uniform pieces for sod-house construction. I had always assumed a plow was used for this job.

The exhibit not only features boom-to-bust eras, dust storms, the World Wars, suitcase farmers, Roosevelt, and more, but it connects events with the lives of real men and women. It alludes to the impact of the telephone, mail routes, the big tractors

busting sod, and the combine.

Finally the exhibit deals with the philosophy of the family farm. Here are a few quotations from the exhibit:

"In 1986 a *New York Times* poll reported that 58% of Americans believed that farm life is more honest and moral than elsewhere. Rural life is Americana."

"Family farmers have the lowest operational costs of any size farming unit and the typical farmer has the skill of a dozen trades."

"There is more at stake than economic efficiency. As farms fail, rural communities deteriorate."

Colby is a great place to explore while enjoying good accommodations on I-70. Don't forget to bring your shopping list for the factory-direct specials, and do drive downtown to appreciate Colby, *the Oasis on the Plains.*

Columbus

Discover Columbus—The Natives Are Friendly

"Help America Discover Columbus." This slogan is an invitation for you from the friendly natives of Columbus, Cherokee County, Kansas. Unlike its namesake, you don't need three sailing ships and soldiers dressed in armor for your exploration. All you need is a desire to relax and discover, and possibly a tank of gas and a credit card.

Cherokee County offers rugged adventure in a wilderness every bit as wild as that which Christopher Columbus faced in the new world. The fact is, hunting might well be better in Cherokee County than where Columbus landed. The fifteenth-century explorer would have felt at home with the area's fine Italian cuisine, but he would have been totally taken aback by an iron monster named for his countryman.

Columbus is a city on the move. That's obvious in just a short drive down Main Street and a talk with one of the forces behind the progress, Jean Pritchett. Jean is the manager of the Columbus Chamber of Commerce. She's a well of enthusiasm and a great resource for visitors. She showed me a mural next to her office which says a lot about the community. The mural, entitled "Achievements of Our Forefathers," depicts a late-1800s scene in which agriculture and industry are working in harmony.

Sometimes it's the simple things that offer the greatest pleasure. I happened by the town's famous clock tower at noon. What excitement! You see, the clock, a rare 1919 Seth Thomas, is encased in glass down on ground level, so you can watch the wooden pendulum swinging exactly one stroke per second. On the hour, all the gears, ratchets, and fans merrily whir as the great bell strikes. The clock at one time was on top of the courthouse.

I enjoyed roaming the 1880s town square, peeking into shops, and admiring the architecture and its vivid coats of many colors. As is true in most towns, the museum helped me gain a historical perspective of the community I was exploring.

So how about something really spectacular, like a sky full of colorful hot air balloons? Columbus, naturally, celebrates Columbus Day every year in October, and the feature event is the hot-air balloon regatta.

Maybe you'd prefer something serene, like a still-water canoe trip in placid cool waters, watching deer, wild turkey, and songbirds of all kinds as you leisurely float along; or the adventure of hunting for deer, turkey, or dove, or fishing for the big ones in some of Kansas's wildest fishing holes.

I needed some background before I appreciated or could

A "strip-pit" lake scene at Mosler's Resort near Hallowell

even believe the uniqueness of Cherokee County's wildlife areas. This region, called the Cherokee Lowlands, was slightly rolling prairie land adapted to agriculture prior to the coal-mining era. Coal mining started here in the late 1800s, but it was not until strip mining replaced shaft mining that the terrain of the whole area changed drastically. Great power shovels opened up coal veins as deep as sixty feet, stripping away all the earth so the coal could be removed.

Near Columbus is Big Brutus, the world's second-largest coal shovel. It weighs in at eleven million pounds and is a "must" attraction. When you see it, you'll understand how flat prairie land could be changed into a hunting and fishing paradise. (Some say there are about two thousand lakes up to sixty feet deep in Cherokee County.)

Big Brutus is now a mining museum and a tribute to the coal miners of a time gone by. Brutus's statistics are awesome: lift capacity 150 tons (enough to fill three railroad cars), 160 feet tall, digging depth sixty feet... and it took 150 railroad cars to deliver the pieces to build Brutus.

Brutus started digging in May of 1963 and continued to do so twenty-four hours a day till April of 1974. It moved only eleven miles in its short career at a

Big Brutus, now a visitor-friendly museum

maximum speed of .22 miles per hour. Brutus and many similar but smaller shovels literally plowed substantial parts of Cherokee and Crawford Counties to a depth of sixty feet. Today some of the land has been reclaimed as pasture, but much of it remains a haphazard wilderness of hills and pits covered with a luxuriant green canopy of trees, bushes, and grasses.

Brutus is visitor-friendly; about thirty thousand people visit annually. For the thrill of your life, follow the steps all the way up. I was going to climb to the top, but daughter Marci was with me and we decided we needed a picture of someone up there. Since I was the better photographer (that day), I reluctantly offered to stay on the ground and take the picture. Marci said it was fun to look down at the pigeons flying far below. Camping, R.V. hookups, and picnicking facili-

ties are available here.

The Kansas Department of Wildlife and Parks owns and operates 14,500 acres of what is known as the Mined Land Wildlife Area, most of which is accessible to the public for fishing, hunting, canoeing, bird-watching, and horsebacking. I soon discovered that a good Mined Lands map was absolutely essential to finding my way around such a vast area. There are also many privately owned strip pit areas (the common name for strip-mined land).

For an introduction to the strip pits, I suggest the Mosler Resort, a rustic facility with cabins, R.V. hookups, fishing, and lots of privacy for swimming and sunbathing. The place is great for reunions, parties, and other gatherings. Lennie Mosler is a professional hunting guide. Across the road, the Claythorne Lodge provides clay-target sports, archery, hunting, and fishing. It bills itself as the ultimate business retreat. You'll enjoy either place, whether you are an avid sportsperson or a novice needing help.

Josie's Ristorante and Lounge in Scammon is my favorite place for Italian food. I like the place twice as much because it's such an unexpected delight in an old coal-mining town with a population of only 475.

Discover Columbus; you'll find a new world.

Concordia
The Stained-Glass Capital of Kansas

It's the people. It's definitely the people that make exploring Concordia so great. Of course, it's easy to say that when you get to have coffee with two charming ladies backstage at the Brown Grand Theatre. Susie Haver and Wonda Brunkow not only make frequent stage appearances, they are also manager and treasurer of the Grand and are part of the noted Susie and the LuWondas Kansas explorer threesome.

The beautifully restored Brown Grand Theatre of Concordia

The Brown Grand ambience is overpowering, sweeping you back to a time when art and elegance were more appreciated. Its great proscenium arch, gracefully molded and sparkling with gold-leaf luster, draws the eye to the vast performing-arts stage. Three tiers of seating—orchestra level, balcony level, and the gallery—provide plush chairs for 650. In true opera-house style, handsome box seats cling to the sides. In honor of the theater's original patron, Colonel Napoleon Bonaparte Brown, a magnificent stage curtain depicts the Emperor Napoleon in his glory at Austerlitz.

Since opening night in 1907 when the Brown Grand's lights first blazed, their radiance has dimmed as depressions and tornadoes have taken their toll, but a recent loving restoration has brought the bright lights back. Susie and her entourage of committees, showpeople, and helpers bring about seventy events annually to north central Kansas. Tours of the theater are offered, and it's a good place to start your exploration of Concordia.

Susie told me that the Kansas Senate has designated Cloud County as the Stained Glass Capital of Kansas. I had thought that stained-glass work was an ancient art, but it is alive and thriving here. You may see glass artists at work in Concordia and take guided or self-guided tours of stained-glass art displayed in churches, homes, and businesses in Concordia, Clyde, St. Joseph, Aurora, Miltonvale, and Jamestown.

Later, after gobbling a sinfully delectable sweet roll at Bobbie and Dot's, I discovered Wellspring, a gift shop featuring local artwork. Linda Chubback Johnson showed me around. This is one of those delightful places where you can watch artists at work; while I was there, Linda was creating a stained-glass piece. Paintings by Cher Olson and weaving by Ann Haritatos are featured.

I've been writing a lot about the "new eyes" Kansas explores need, but artists must see things in even another way. Cher had just painted an antique chair. It was very lovely, but the seat was split. This old farmer would have nailed a plywood top over it before painting it. Cher preferred to retain its flaws; perhaps they tell a story.

I had a nice talk with Larry Blochlinger, president of the Concordia Chamber of Commerce. Larry mentioned that earlier in his career he and his family had lived in Kansas City.

"We didn't lose anything by moving to a smaller town," he said. "The children actually have more opportunities here. The security... we can let kids play outside here." Larry was another friendly Concordian proud of his community and anticipating a great future. Concordia is a delightful town—prosperous, clean, safe, with lots of cuisine and lodging options.

Then I met Brad Chapin; now here is a man that lives in the past. I mean that kindly, because it's obvious he thinks the past has a lot to say about the future. Brad is the curator of the Cloud County Historical Museum. His enthusiasm was high, and no wonder. The new annex, with a rare Lincoln-Page airplane suspended from the ceiling, is outstanding. This well-lit, spacious structure displays everything from anvils to windmills. Included in the displays are an 1898 Holsman belt-driven horseless carriage with a five-horsepower motor under the seat, a complete 1900s kitchen, military items, a blacksmith shop complete with a lineshaft, a McCormick reaper,

and more than sixty-five horse-drawn implements, most of them field ready. In one corner of the annex you'll find a twenty-by-forty-foot peg barn. Timbers with mortised joints locked together with oak pegs form the framework.

Very unusual is a display of prisoner-of-war memorabilia. During World War II about forty-five thousand German prisoners were quartered several miles north of Concordia. A garrison of 815 American soldiers guarded them. Little of the camp remains: a rebuilt guard tower, a large concrete water-tower base, a few wooden buildings, and local memories. I was reminded here that it's easy for an explorer to jump to false conclusions. Far into the field is a steel observation tower; it once overlooked a race track of later vintage.

Out in the countryside north

of Rice (not on the map, it's east of Concordia) is a small stone-arch bridge. Once on the main road between Concordia and Clyde, it's now on a dead-end path. It's refreshing to see that this outmoded relic is obviously treasured by many. Perfectly restored, it just sits there under a huge cottonwood waiting for an old Model T Ford or a Maxwell to rumble across its floor on the road to nowhere. You'll gain a few moments of serenity by exploring it.

Many miles south on an isolated road stands a tribute to Boston Corbett, the soldier who shot John Wilkes Booth after he assassinated President Lincoln. Corbett is said to have lived in a dugout sixty feet south of the monument in 1878.

The puzzling evolution of Kansas small towns is apparent in the rest of Cloud County: Clyde appears to be a prospering full-service town (you'll love the food in the picturesque Van DeMark House). Jamestown is a paradox—some very nice homes, Main Street virtually abandoned (with a few exceptions, including a post office and a bank), and a population decline of thirty percent in twenty years. The rest of the towns seem to be declining (even the magnificent Catholic church in St. Joseph is closed). My hope is that you will visit these towns and ponder the changes in your heart.

Restored stone-arch bridge near Rice

Cottonwood Falls
Flint Hills Brigadoon

For your first journey here follow the Cowboy Trail from Elmdale to Cottonwood Falls. Block out the trees, power lines, and blacktop. Let the Flint Hills mesmerize you; let your new eyes see the hills as they were in 1873—an undulating carpet of tall bluestem, Indian grass, and myriad wildflowers. Listen to ancient echoes—wagon wheels rumble and bounce on rock, horses snort, and harness jangles—and let the winds of yesterday caress your face.

David and Brenda Kirk welcome you to Jim Bell & Son, Inc.

When you reach Cottonwood Falls, turn south on Broadway. Like a medieval castle guarding its village, the Chase County courthouse dominates the town. Surprisingly French in appearance, the white limestone walls, red mansard roof topped with a cupola, iron grill widow's walk, and thirty-foot flagpole present an idyllic image.

Inside, the storybook illusion continues. A massive spiral stairway and black walnut balustrade extend from the entry to the third floor. A somber second-floor courtroom and adjoining iron jail reflect the justice dispatched here since 1873, when the courthouse was completed. This courthouse, the oldest still in use in Kansas, is open weekdays and weekend afternoons to visitors.

Peering from an oval window on the third level you see the town's main street, Broadway, far below, almost too charming to be real. It *is* real, however.

Cottonwood Falls is a working cattle town, the county seat of Chase County, intimately chronicled by author William Least Heat Moon in *PrairyErth*.

The charm of Cottonwood Falls is its authenticity. The buildings and streets, many a century old or more, reveal the strong and fiercely independent character of early and contemporary citizens. The renewal of Cottonwood Falls is not a slavish restoration of detail but rather a rebirth of its original vibrancy.

The newest revival of the old is the Grand Central Hotel. Built in 1884 and totally renovated in 1995, the Grand is advertised as enhancing Old West elegance with New World hospitality. Each of the ten oversized rooms is "branded" with a local historical brand. The aura of the West prevails, but jacuzzi/sauna showers, cable television, and king and queen beds dispel any fears of pioneer discomfort. Fine dining is offered to hotel guests and the public.

Down the street, Jim Bell and Son, a chic western-wear store, is simply astounding. Here, in a town of fewer than eight hundred people, is a store that attracts a host of shoppers from Wichita, Kansas City, Tulsa—in fact, glancing at the guest book, I saw names of visitors from all over the world. On just one page I noted addresses in Scotland, Canada, Japan, Arizona, Oklahoma, and many other far-flung locations.

The store was remodeled in 1993. Ahead of its time architecturally when it was built in 1902, the unorthodox one-hundred-percent concrete structural design permitted discrete columns to support an open mezzanine. Today brass railings around the mezzanine and an open stairway provide startling elegance unexpected in a small town.

Manager David Kirk says,

"We found our niche in the marketplace and it's working very well. We matched our product line to the western traditions and charisma of the Flint Hills and Cottonwood Falls."

The spacious, rolling Flint Hills grandeur is so obvious that it sometimes masks a subtle and mysterious essence that can touch the soul. Flint Hills artist Judy Mackey captures that mystique on canvas. Two mounted cowboys, a windmill, and a far horizon poignantly depict a reality far beyond the stress of our daily lives. Judy welcomes visitors to her studio, the Flint Hills Gallery. Watch her at work and consider taking a bit of the hills home with you.

Judy's studio, some agricultural service offices, and various professional buildings on Broadway are all early structures that have been carefully restored to an attractive and functional condition. Lavish use of oak in doors and trim is a hallmark of the "new" Cottonwood Falls. This town is an example of recycling at its best. Further down the block an old armory has been converted to a Duckwall's store.

Specialty shops, the kind visitors love to browse, are indeed a pleasant surprise. Prairie Rose offers gifts, antiques, and flowers. Brenda Bruch, the proprietor, is always delighted to talk about Cottonwood Falls. Across the street the Fiber Factory expands on the recycling concept. Carol and Charley Klamm use turn-of-the-century looms to weave rugs, place mats, blankets, and shawls out of discarded blue jeans. It's fun to watch this old technology at work—slam bang, a pattern emerges.

And then there is Professor Bones. I honestly don't think he minds being called a rather unusual character. You'll find him at the Cotton Wood Works on Broadway. He's an entertainer, a restorer of antique furniture, an entrepreneur, and above all a lot of fun. Right now he's into making puzzles—the hundred-piece kind featuring landmarks like the Chase County Courthouse and the Z-Bar Ranch.

The Chase County Courthouse, oldest courthouse in Kansas

To rub shoulders with the local citizens, stop in at the new Emma Chase Restaurant. Don't expect to meet the stereotypical cracker-barrel provincials in Cottonwood Falls or, for that matter, in any of our rural Kansas communities. The "locals" may be cowboys, attorneys, artists, farmers, clerks, retirees, or senators, but they are all distinct, diverse individuals doing their jobs. Most are willing to share a little bit of their life stories. Some may not; an explorer is discreet enough to know. Be sure to ask about Emma Chase; she's quite a conversation piece.

Harder's Market is difficult to classify. The hometown atmosphere is there, a pressed-tin ceiling peeks through a hole in a false ceiling, but computers have found their way in as well. Owners Ken and Jeri Harder also are a great Kansas travel information resource. They publish the monthly *Kansas Tour Guide*. On the other hand, not even a telephone has invaded Tall Grass Gallery, where Ken Mackey makes bootjacks, belt buckles, spurs, and you name it. If you want to experience the hills, check out the 1874 Stonehouse Bed-and-Breakfast. It's only a few miles out of town, and it's ideal for those who love nature *and* comfort.

Cottonwood Falls will capture your heart any season of the year.

Council Grove
Next Stop, Santa Fe

COUNCIL GROVE, LOUISIANA TERRITORY, 1825, the grove of oaks where Osage chiefs and U.S. commissioners negotiated a trail to Santa Fe.

COUNCIL GROVE, KANSAS TERRITORY, 1857, where Seth Hays and Tom Hill built the Hays House and the Last Chance Store alongside the Santa Fe Trail.

COUNCIL GROVE, KANSAS, 1996, the place where memories of an old trail, the enduring land of hills and rivers, and the spirits of diverse people long buried resonate in the life of a thriving city.

On the surface, exploring Council Grove was so easy that it belies the word *exploring*. Eighteen points of interest are mapped and marked for the modern explorer, but I soon discovered that there was always a story behind the story. At the Hays House, stop number ten, the sign says, "Oldest restaurant west of the Mississippi, established 1857."

The cuisine at the Hays House, now owned and operated by Rick and Alisa Paul, is the best—Flint Hills steaks and homemade breads, soups, and desserts—but that's not all that piqued my interest. The heavy wood timbers in the main dining room and the rough-cut beams and limestone walls in the cellar luncheon nook had been there when sweaty drovers cursing at oxen and mules went by on the dusty Santa Fe Trail. Within these walls Jesse James and George Armstrong Custer plotted and planned. (Too bad Jesse and George missed Alisa and Rick's Saturday night prime rib special.)

A good place to start your Council Grove explorations is at interest point number one, the Kaw Mission, circa 1851. A curator will tell you of the Indians' tragic decline and the white man's successful quest for domination. You'll see maps and relevant period artifacts. Area information is available here.

So it goes. Each stop has a story to tell: The Post Office Oak and the Last Chance speak of the lonely, hostile trail ahead. The Madonna of the Trail statue honors the courage of pioneer women. The Old Calaboose recalls frontier justice, and a stone barn built in 1871 symbolizes the end of the trail era.

A happy synthesis of old and new is the Cottage House Hotel, point of interest number six. The hotel dates back to 1867, with additions in 1898, 1908, and 1913. All the modern comforts are found in each room, but the historical integrity has been maintained. Sleeping in a room where frontiersmen and pioneer immigrants once rested gives me a sense of being part of history.

You can see evidence of the Santa Fe Trail, stop five, about five miles west of town. It wasn't quite what I expected. There are no wagon-wheel ruts. Instead I found a swale twenty to thirty feet wide formed by wagon wheels, hooves, and erosion. In places there are parallel swales where wagons drove side by side or where the trail was moved out of a dusty track to a grassy area.

Yearning for farm life of bygone days? I found remnants of stone fences and old stone houses and barns as I drove on country roads south and west of the Santa Fe Trail swales. Sadly,

The Canopy—old-fashioned soda fountain window service

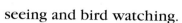

The Hays House, there since the Santa Fe Trail era

I noted that at least three out of four farmsteads are abandoned. Enjoy driving by; this is all private property.

Back in Council Grove is more evidence of the Santa Fe Trail. Riffles in the Neosho River bed just north of the Main Street bridge show where the trail crossed the river on hard rock. And notice how the Hays House is set back from Main at a slight angle. It was built parallel to the original trail, while the rest of town was built later at a different orientation.

Thirsty drovers and pioneers of the trail era would have appreciated Aldrich Apothecary's old-fashioned soda fountain. You can relax with a friend and sip cool green rivers, cherry phosphates, or sarsaparilla. Ice cream tastes great at the marble bar where swivel stools and a brass foot rail bring back the good old days. In the summertime you can place your order outside under a little blue canopy.

Council Grove, tucked in the Neosho River Valley, is surrounded by the famed Flint Hills of Kansas. Highway K-177, a north-south route through the heart of the Flint Hills and the city, has been designated from Council Grove to Cassoday as the first Kansas Scenic Byway. Scenery and panoramic views have been computer-evaluated and classified by the Kansas Department of Transportation. An attractive scenic-byways logo on signs calls attention to highway attractions. The famed Z Bar Ranch and the Lower Fox Creek School are included on this route.

Highway U.S. 56, known as the Santa Fe Trail Road, runs east-west through Council Grove, fairly well following the original trail across town as it does all the way from Kansas City southwest to Elkhart. Deep road cuts just east of town reveal the limestone layers found throughout the Flint Hills.

If it's water recreation and sports you enjoy, it's all here at Council Grove Lake northwest of the city. This federal reservoir offers swimming, boating, water-skiing, camping, picnicking, fishing, and hunting. The natural diversity, wooded coves, open water, crop and pasture land, and prairie hills make this a great place for sightseeing and bird watching.

If you have a boat, exploring the upper reaches of the old river and creek beds is a lot of fun. Trees reaching across the channels lead you to an almost primeval neverland. To see the rolling beauty of the hills, journey along the western shore where you'll see the natural terrain, uncluttered by trees, as it appeared when bison and prairie fires gave the tall grasses and flowers a competitive edge.

A picturesque setting for upscale homes and summer cottages is found at nearby Council Grove City Lake. Arriving from the east, with morning light at your back, you'll see a charming little village edging the shore across the water.

The list of exploration possibilities continues to grow in Council Grove. A new walkway along the Neosho River begins at the Main Street bridge just across the road from the Madonna of the Trail statue and continues up the river and across to the Kaw Mission. The Kaw Warrior, a new bronze statue at the walkway entrance, pays tribute to the Kaw (Kansa) people who lived in this region 150 years before Kansas statehood.

A Council Grove tour should be a part of every Kansan's education. Family members of all ages will find much to enjoy and remember in an exploration of this historic frontier gateway.

Dighton

Fireflies and the Aroma of Fresh-Cut Straw

Dighton? Lane County? Where in the world is that... and why in the world would I want to go there?

Well, I'll tell you why. In Dighton and its environs you'll encounter a way of life that seems nearly extinct or at the very least provincial. Yet this "way of life" is what a frustrated America is seeking to recapture. Citizens here do not flaunt their virtues; they express their values by simply being what they are....

This is wheat country, and harvest was in full swing. Trucks carrying huge green harvest machines, with occasional reds and silvers, streamed through town on K-96, many stopping to unload at the Dighton fairgrounds. This friendly legion annually hop-scotches from wheat fields in Texas to the wheat provinces of Canada. No nine-to-five lightweights need apply here for work. The crew may roll into a new destination at dusk, but as soon as the combines are unloaded and cutter platforms attached they roll into the fields to cut wheat at night till the dewpoint reaches a critical stage.

An attractive building on a corner caught my eye. The gold letters on the door read "Old Bank Gallery." Inside, watercolor artist Patrycia Herndon was bending over an easel, brush in hand. Looking over her shoulder I saw the drama of a cattle auction at a sale barn develop on paper—the animated auctioneer, the confused pen of cattle, the cool nod of a buyer. Pat was just back from displaying her colorful interpretation of Lane County's way of life at Wichita's Botanica, and it was obvious she loved that way of life. She talked of life qualities: the joy of work, harmony, security, community pride. Her art expresses another wonderful quality: the ability to see beauty and drama in the mundane.

Pat did a wonderful job of preserving the integrity of the old First National Bank building when she converted it into her studio. The restored tellers' cages now graciously receive deposits on Pat's watercolors.

Pat suggested lunch. "Fine," I said, "but where do you go for lunch in Dighton?" She took me next door to what looked like an abandoned warehouse. Surprise! "Warm," "cozy," "western" would describe the decor. Suspended from the high ceiling was an authentic spring wagon—bright green box, red wheels. As we discussed the circa 1906 building, I heard stories of operas, traveling shows, and finally movies upstairs and a mercantile store on the lower level.

Maybe it was the Lane County

Custom combines arriving for the wheat harvest in Dighton

encounters with the unexpect-ed elements of rural culture that I enjoyed so much. I was traveling along K-4 near Shields when I saw a modest little white sign saying "Cat House Rec" and an arrow pointing north. What would *you* have expected? Cautious as I am, I went back to Dighton to check this out with Pat. She laughed, reached for her phone, and made an appointment for me to meet Trula at two in the after-noon at the Cat House Rec gate.

Wow! Eleven hundred acres of rolling green hills, blue-water lakes impounded by small dams, white cliffs, chalky buttes, eigh-teen buffalo-grass golf greens, and miles and miles of tortuous white roads, plus corrals for team-penning events. This is western Kansas? Trula drove me through the resort, enthusiasti-cally recounting how she, hus-band Clayton Davis, and ranch hands built up the area because they enjoyed doing it. When you meet the Davises, ask them to explain the name.

Another surprise was a real sod house at the Lane County Museum. The museum depicts the Lane County way of life in pioneer days. A sod dugout; an ox yoke; plows; pioneer furni-ture; and pictures of schools, churches, and fine early build-ings on Main Street testify to hard work and a quest for excel-lence and self-sufficiency. A few

Artist Patrycia Herndon in her Old Bank Gallery

stops downtown assured me that these values persevere.

Recorded music played on a street corner, an old hotel was being renovated, shops and stores were busy. In the drug store at coffee time, people were cordial and conversant. Typically, Barb Newberry, owner of Fond Memories Antiques, was proud of her store, proud of Dighton; and she made me, a visitor, feel wel-come in town.

After a drink at the Quick Shop, another one of those local gathering places, I discovered that my mini-van was dead—no starter, no lights. "It's close to closing time," I thought. "Where will I get help at this time of day?" A helpful police-man directed me to nearby J and D Service. I ran over there; he obviously was busy, but see-

ing my concern he came right out to help. To make a long story short, he worked over-time to get me going again, and he was happy to do it.

Later I drove to the local grain elevator to photograph grain trucks unloading. A middle-aged woman drove up in a large truck carrying about three hundred bushels of wheat. While waiting to unload, she told me they'd finally been able to get the com-bine into the wet fields.

After sundown, I drove out into the country, watching combine lights, almost like fire-flies, moving in the fields. I could hear the diesel engines laboring, occasionally throt-tling down as the operator shifted gears to back out of a wet spot. I could feel the chaff floating in the air and smell the fresh-cut straw.

I recapped my day in Dighton. Nothing really drama-tic had happened, but some-thing about the calm, assured demeanor of the woman driving the wheat truck brought the Dighton story together. The people I had met went about doing their jobs well, assured in their sense of community and freely sharing their bliss.

I discovered the essence of Dighton by becoming involved with its people—lunch, sharing, shopping, business, repair, and conversation. The Dighton way of life is genuine Americana.

Dodge City
The Legend of the One Hundredth Meridian

One hundred seventy-five years ago, at the point where the hundredth meridian and the Arkansas River intersect, the river flowed wide and free upon its sandy bed, seldom disturbed except for an occasional deer or antelope. From a natural perspective there was nothing unusual about this place, but its location at one hundred degrees west longitude on the white man's charts made it a good spot for the corner of a military reservation.

In 1821 United States government surveyors and eager traders had begun following the river's northern bank on their way to Santa Fe. When Fort Dodge was built in 1865, its northwest corner was at the hundredth meridian, where it met the river.

Today the Arkansas River seldom flows there, but this magical intersection has become the stuff of legends. Throughout the world the name of Dodge City brings to mind images of grim lawmen—stern eyes shaded by big cowboy hats—and smoking six-guns, and, in the background, the starkness of Boot Hill. Visitors from all over the world—Japanese, Germans, Spaniards—parade daily through Boot Hill Museum awed by the deadly human dramas that occurred here. In early Dodge City the tumultuous excitement of the Santa Fe Trail, the Indian Wars, the buffalo hunters, the building of the railroad, and the Texas cattle drives was crunched into two decades.

Dodge City celebrates the legend. Infamous Front Street is back and thriving again. Stagecoaches creak and bounce, Miss Kitty and her Can Can Girls perform, and lawmen shoot down outlaws daily.

The Boot Hill Museum is open throughout the year. During visitor season on the carefully replicated Front Street, thousands of visitors vicariously experience Dodge City's gory glory days as actors daily re-enact the stirring events. The Dodge City, Ford & Bucklin excursion and dinner trains let you experience the era when rails opened up the West.

What's behind the drama of Dodge City? That's what I set out to explore, and I found the truth as exciting as the legend.

It all started with the Santa Fe Trail. Creaking along slowly at first, traffic on the trail gained momentum. Soon over a million dollars worth of goods annually moved along the trail, and Fort Dodge was built to protect the travelers from Indians. Here

Replicated Front Street near Dodge City's Boot Hill

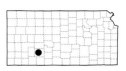

El Capitan sculpture, Stan Herd mural in background

today, many trail points of interest, including original fort buildings and wagon ruts, are noted by site markers. Special events will celebrate the Santa Fe Trail's 175th anniversary in 1996.

Originally the sale of whiskey was prohibited on the Fort Dodge Military Reservation. In 1872, when the railroad neared the fort, a young Canadian named George Hoover tied a handkerchief around a wagon wheel and measured five miles to determine the fort's western boundary, which approximated the hundredth meridian. On June 17, 1875, he set up shop there with a wagonload of whiskey to sell to parched track layers. The site would become Dodge City, just a step beyond the law, and George Hoover would become one of the most influential men in Dodge City's history.

The town grew rambunctiously. Buffalo hunters followed the iron horse. In only two years the buffalo had been exterminated, to be replaced by longhorn cattle from Texas. Thus one wave of lonely, law-less men followed another, giving rise to the Dodge City legend until cattle quarantine laws, blizzards, and homesteaders brought the era to an end and Turkey Red wheat, introduced by Russian Mennonites, vanquished the lawless. Ever since, agriculture and related commerce have dominated the thriving Dodge City region.

Old Dodge City's cattle-town era may have been more glamorous, but current cattle statistics are staggering. From a hill-top east of the city a visitor can see three modern feedlots spread out below. Old-timers talk of three thousand cattle in one herd on the trail; here you can see up to fifty thousand cattle on one hillside. Giant trucks haul seventy or more cattle down the road at sixty miles an hour; 750 "pots" hauling fifty thousand pounds of live cattle per load service Dodge City.

Everything seems large in Dodge City, even the art. A mural hundreds of feet long painted across the front and sides of the Hy Plains Beef Packing Plant greets travelers coming into town on K-154. A vast Arkansas River Valley landscape reveals the collage of events that created Dodge City's fascinating history. World-renowned artist Stan Herd introduces Coronado's band crossing the Arkansas River and concludes the pictorial saga with Texas cowboys celebrating in the streets of Dodge City.

Downtown, above the city and larger than life, dashing horses and a stagecoach charge out of another Herd mural painted on the First National Bank building—a very dramatic sight from a few blocks south.

Dodge City's gracious accommodations and friendly people make experiencing the legend a pleasure. Restaurants, lodging, entertainment, services, shopping, parks—it's all there, and the red carpet is always rolled out for visitors. The Dodge City Convention and Visitors Bureau is there to help, providing trolley rides, informative cassettes keyed to points of interest, guide maps, and other information.

As I followed the walking-tour brochure I became aware of another side of Dodge City—Gospel Hill, for example, a hill-top where a succession of churches and cathedrals have looked down on the once-wicked streets below. The architecture of the churches and civic buildings in the area is eclectic, ranging from Spanish Mission to Italian Renaissance, and a unique 1907 Carnegie Library now houses a center for the arts.

"Eclectic," in fact, is a good word to describe Dodge City. The legend may be fascinating, but diversity and prosperity describe the present and future here on the hundredth meridian.

Doniphan County
Abraham Lincoln Slept Here

In Troy, the Doniphan County seat, I checked in at Sheila's Cafe. Pickup trucks parked outside told me it was men's coffee hour, and coffee-cup wisdom was being freely dispensed. I was there to meet George Jorgensen, a retired District Soil Conservationist, who volunteered to show me the early and earthy history of Doniphan County.

After George and I chatted at Sheila's for a while, we drove to an overlook two hundred feet above the Missouri River in the extreme northeast corner of Kansas. Pointing north to Nebraska and Iowa he explained how an ice age glacier and subsequent climactic dust storms formed the hills of Doniphan County. I could envision an ice bulldozer a mile high pushing the best of the Nebraska soil south and depositing it in Kansas. "Now," George said, "these highly productive loess hills are known as Little Switzerland."

In White Cloud, just below this vantage point, we met Wolf River Bob, a flamboyant ex-Hollywood stunt man. Bob helps produce one of the largest flea-market extravaganzas in a four-state area. Up to twenty thousand people come to White Cloud and nearby Sparks and Troy in early May and late September. If Bob's around when you visit White Cloud, ask him to show you the Lewis and Clark Lookout high above the river. Bob is moving an 1867 log cabin up there piece by piece, and his enthusiastic stories will enthrall you.

On the way back from White Cloud, George asked me if I liked old barns. "You bet," I said. For me, barns stir warm memories of new-mown alfalfa, of tumbling from a hayloft mountain, and of milking shorthorns by the light of a kerosene lantern. So we went barn-hopping. Doniphan County has an unusual number of old byre and bluff barns (1860 to 1933) on the National Register of Historic Places. Self-guided tour maps are available.

Back in Troy, George pointed out a house where Abe Lincoln purportedly slept during a presidential campaign trip into Kansas. Not many houses in Kansas are old enough to make that claim. (It's the little white house just north of the courthouse.)

I left George at Sheila's just in time for afternoon coffee (same pick-ups, same conversation recharged by a dose of radio talk shows). I went down the street to Nelson Pharmacy because I'd heard they had the medicine I needed, an old-time soda fountain. Mike Nelson, the owner, told me that during repair work they had found a board with carpenters' autographs dated 1871. Elbows on the marble counter, sipping a cherry phosphate, I felt connected with a time long ago.

Later, under heavy clouds, I drove south where the spirit led me. I spotted another unique barn, this time an octagonal one somewhere near Denton, and in Denton I found a hand pump in the middle of the main intersection. Camera in hand, I was wondering whether or not the pump worked when a friendly gentleman came out of the bank, pumped the handle, and water gushed out. I asked to take a picture and he beat a hasty retreat.

Wolf River Bob on a bluff overlooking the Missouri River

Tall Oak, Native American monument sculpted from an oak tree

A bolt of lightning pointed to a steeple miles ahead. I followed a country road and discovered the shortest state highway in Kansas, K-137. (I "discovered" it in the same sense that Columbus "discovered" America—the natives knew it was there all along.) It's at Purcell, population zero except when church is in session. K-137 goes south from K-20 almost two-tenths of a mile to end at a farmyard.

Raindrops splashed on the windshield as I headed for Doniphan, a ghost town on the other side of the county. Ghosts don't need blacktop, so the road was gravel all the way. Inhabitants are sparse; the county peaked in 1900, and population has been on the decline ever since.

The hollow, vacant stare of an abandoned mercantile store in Doniphan is a haunting reminder of the hustle and bustle of the town's glory days. I shiver every time I see it. Doniphan was a major river steamboat port until a flood moved the Missouri River a mile east. A steamboat, the *Salley*—three decks, rear paddle wheel, two hundred feet long—hit a river snag October 22, 1869, and sank near Doniphan. The channel change left the boat under forty feet of river mud. Efforts will be made to raise the *Salley* in 1996. Talk about ghosts.

Light rain made me uneasy as I headed northeast along the river. Since I had no idea where the road would take me, the unknown miles seemed longer and longer. Finally, to my relief and surprise, an old river town appeared ahead. That first glimpse of Wathena from the south captures the town as it was over a hundred years ago; the buildings are still there and in daily use. The old bank building is now a cafe, so stop for a

Old mercantile building in ghost town of Doniphan

bite in the Taste of Country.

The next morning, to my dismay, I found the State Historical Society's Native American Museum near Highland closed and in the process of expansion. A few days later I had a delightful telephone conversation with Suzette Rogers, the new curator. She told me about exciting things they'll have for visitors in the Native American Heritage Museum: Native American folk art, European folk art, Native American history, hands-on workshops for children, Oregon Trail swales, ghost town tours, and more. I must go back when it reopens in 1996.

Native Americans are a very vital part of Doniphan County culture, but to the casual explorer they appear to be assimilated into mainstream society. Apart from other contributions, they provide entertainment—first-class rodeos, pow-wows, and bingo—for the public. Many prefer not to have their culture under closer scrutiny, and it's important to respect that.

A giant tribute to Native Americans, Tall Oak, is on the Doniphan County courthouse lawn in Troy. Sculpted by Peter Toth out of bur oak, this twenty-seven-foot monument is one of a series of "Whispering Giants" found in every state.

I found great diversity and delight in Doniphan County; I'm sure you will too.

Elk Falls

A Rooster's Call at Dawn

Elk Falls, population 120, bills itself as a living ghost town, but ghosts labeled "Fast Lane" and "Avarice" left a long time ago. It's obvious, however, that the spirits of inner peace, joy, and compassion abide.

I have visited Elk Falls many times; each time I leave, I'm inspired and troubled. It's refreshing to see a lifestyle almost naively simple, authentic, and honest. Words like rustic, pastoral, and idyllic come to mind, but to experience the charm you must meet the people. Without the spirit that the people voice, the town appears as an empty shell, and that's what troubles me. Elk Falls is a state of mind, and I don't know if I could ever let go of material goals as completely as its citizens do.

Barry McGuire is the driving force behind "touristy" Elk Falls. Barry, a retired actor, has appeared on television shows such as "Father Knows Best," "The Real McCoys," "Gunsmoke," and "Perry Mason," and in his little Elk Falls Variety Theatre you'll find a picture of him skating cheek to cheek with Debbie Reynolds in a movie. He responded to an ad extolling the virtues of Elk Falls, fell in love with the town, and decided to adopt its lifestyle.

Barry's first project in Elk Falls was a delightful floral garden built over and around a burned-out home. Quotations from the Bible, Gilbert and Sullivan, and Shakespeare adorn the garden's Path of Wisdom. As the garden began to attract many visitors the tourism idea

Steve Fry, Elk Falls Pottery, "throwing" a stoneware vessel

developed. Today Barry and Margery Cunningham, both dressed in period costumes, host tour buses in Elk Falls— limit one per day.

You'll know you're at Elk Falls Pottery when you see a red "stop" sign that says "POTS." Steve and Jane Fry discovered Elk Falls by answering the same ad that attracted Barry. They bought a house for a thousand dollars, moved it, and remodeled it as a studio and home. Other than a few light bulbs, what you see would have been familiar to early pioneers here. Usually you can find Steve at the foot-powered potter's wheel while Jane does the trimming, and glazing and fires the pottery in the kiln. The Frys welcome visitors and are happy to talk about their art and life in Elk Falls. There is a waiting list for their products.

A few blocks down the street, in a modest but very neat home and garage, Mack Byard does custom tanning as a serious sideline and construction work as a general contractor. Walk into his garage and you walk back to a time when pioneers relied on leather products. Deer, beaver, and elk hides in various stages of progress are all over the place. Most of what you see and smell would have been familiar to residents of Elk Falls a hundred years ago. The inoffensive yet pungent oder of

Barry McGuire's Village Variety Theatre

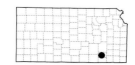

raw animal hides reminds me of how isolated from reality we have become. Mack tells how a woman from Dallas was excited about seeing how leather was made until she discovered it came from from animal hides. Mack says, "Can you imagine an adult not knowing what leather is made of?" It's fascinating to see all the steps involved– fleshing, soaking in different solutions, and stretching.

Of course you must see the falls on the Elk River. It doesn't compare to Niagara Falls, but your "new eyes" will see the ancient stone carved out by eons of water flowing to the ocean. Stop to think how important the everlasting flow of water is to life on earth. At one time a flour mill was perched there beside the river. Remnants of the mill dam are still there. The best vantage point, especially for morning photos, is from a nearby iron truss bridge built in 1893 and now closed to traffic.

I had lunch at the Cape Cod Bakery and Restaurant and I loved it. The food was great, but it's the down-home feeling I remember. The door stuck as I entered; I had to push hard. But the friendly greeting by Rebeka Eck–owner, chef, waitress, and dishwasher–was most welcoming. Barry joined me for lunch and told me about a new fundraising project. I wasn't quite sure whether or not it was tongue-in-cheek (if it was an act, I didn't want him to know he fooled me). He said for a quarter you can pick a rock in the street, they'll put your name on it, and you can deposit it in the chuckhole of your choice.

Part of Elk Falls Americana is a sawmill's big blade screaming through native lumber at the Elk Falls Sawmill. The operator nimbly pushes and pulls levers, and magically clean squared boards emerge amid flying sawdust. Farther down the road the 1872 Keefe Pioneer Homestead bears tribute to the durability of wood frame houses and barns. Visitors may tour this old home furnished as it was many years ago. A guide details its history and role in the County Seat War of 1873.

You'll enjoy Barry's show in his own Village Variety Theatre. (Notice how high-class theaters spell *theater* with an "re.") This venerable building perhaps has always been in a stage of near-completion. It began as a lumber planing mill, then it was a church dining hall, and now it's a quaint theater reminiscent of the 1880s. Barry's one-man vaudeville show features comedy, puppets, magic, and lots of fun.

Authentic architecture and modern comfort converge in the 115-year-old Sherman House Bed-and-Breakfast. Once a railroad stopover, the Sherman House has been cut down in size, moved, and skillfully remodeled by Steve and Jane Fry. Compared to the town's "as it once was" atmosphere, the elegance of this place is stunning. We are planning to take our family there as soon as we can all get together. Sofia and Alyssa will love the Bunkhouse Room, with its tepee, kid-sized tack room, and what looks like a real glowing campfire. The best part of all is waking up with a rooster crowing at dawn and anticipating Jane's delicious breakfast–an array of mouth-watering choices.

Spend a day and a night in Elk Falls. There's nothing like it anywhere.

Elkhart

Perils of the Cimarron Cutoff

It was one hundred and one degrees hot, the noon sun bore straight down, and the buffalo grass was so dry it crunched and crackled under my boots. It was just what I wanted.

I was at Middle Springs on the old Santa Fe Trail, about eight miles north of Elkhart in Morton County. It was lonely country. I'm sure no one else was around for miles, only some chattering western kingbirds and to my surprise an orchard oriole sharing the solitude. One hundred and twenty-five years ago the last wagons came by the spring, and much has changed here through the years; maybe only the heat is the same. I wanted to go back in time for at least a few minutes.

Now the spring is barely running and is surrounded by trees. Later I learned from Joe Hartman, District Ranger of the Cimarron National Grasslands, that during the Santa Fe Trail era there had been no trees. Travelers had chopped up any that might have been there for firewood. Before irrigation pumps lowered the aquifer, Hartman told me, Middle Springs had been a dependable source of water.

I enjoyed my exploration of the grasslands and my stay in Elkhart immensely. The Cimarron National Grasslands may be the most overlooked Kansas treasure. I suspect the Cimarron Cutoff syndrome—dangerous, dry, and desolate—misleads a lot of people. . . keeps them

from coming here to enjoy.

I want to assure you that Elkhart is safe, well watered, and prosperous. It's a very comfortable town: full-service hometown shopping, excellent hospital and care center (eight doctors), outstanding library, thriving businesses, cozy restaurants, and restful lodging. I was impressed by the nice homes, shaded streets, and green lawns. And then there's Whistle Stop Park, probably the longest and narrowest city park in Kansas. It's a surfaced path on an old railroad right-of-way for walking, biking, and roller blading.

Yes, this is southwest Kansas. It gets hot and annual rainfall averages only sixteen inches, but Elkhart copes very well with the elements. The old American

virtues of hard work, responsibility, and self-reliance are alive and well in Morton County. It's a community of survivors, and the National Grasslands story has a lot to say about surviving.

So what are these grasslands and why should you explore them? The Cimarron National Grasslands cover over 108 thousand acres of land devastated by dust storms in the 1930s and restored to its present state by the federal government. Ironically it was a period of prosperity and the development of the farm tractor that turned Morton County into the heart of the Dust Bowl. A good price for wheat after World War I lured high-plains farmers into converting every possible acre of cheap land into wheat fields. When the rains stopped, disaster followed.

A dust storm of 1930s proportions is something you can't describe adequately on paper. Living as a youth in central Kansas I recall only two, but the mark left in my memory is indelible. The upshot was that most Morton County farmers lost everything. The federal government bought back the land (providing enough money for farm families to move away), and began a restoration program. Today with wise management of federal and private lands and mineral production Morton County is doing very well.

The largest display in the

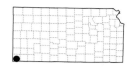

Russell steam tractor, Morton County Museum

Morton County Museum is a huge black and red Russell compound steam tractor, typical of the machines that made plowing the prairies in large tracts possible. No mere horse-and-walking plow could have done the job. I got on the operator's platform and imagined myself driving this ungainly mass of fire-breathing iron across virgin grassland. Stoking coal or wood into the engine's firebox on a hundred-degree day probably made driving a Santa Fe Trail freight wagon seem like a plush job. Most of the sod-busting was done, however, with gasoline tractors of equal proportions.

Exploring the Grasslands is a unique experience. You can stand on top of Point of Rocks and with your new explorer eyes envision the past unfurling below you: a vast grass-covered plain; the Cimarron River hidden under hot sand; buffalo by the thousands; high-wheeled freight wagons pulled by three or four pair of yoked oxen with drovers walking by their sides; the Cimarron River flood of 1914 washing away the Beatty Ranch and killing two children; and utter desolation with only a few yucca spears showing when the Dust Bowl storms subsided.

Exploring is stopping at a creaking windmill and sticking your arms into the cool tank water. It's driving through the Cimarron River without a bridge (on the self-guided tour route). It's digging down into the sand with your hands to find the river.

And it's walking through the sagebrush and prickly pear to see the Santa Fe Trail ruts. Exploring is bird watching—269 species have been identified in the Grasslands.

I'm embarrassed to tell you what happened at my first stop on the self-guided tour. A sign pointed to the "guzzler." I went through a turnstile and couldn't find him or it. All I saw was a dry, low spot and a junky tin roof. Later I was informed that this tin roof *was* the guzzler. It collects morning dew that runs into troughs below. Wildlife—quail, turkeys, turtles, and more—come here for water.

The Grasslands Auto Tour parallels the historic Santa Fe Trail for about twenty-three miles on maintained rock road (good tires are a must). It takes about three hours. Ponder if you will that this drive represents about a day and a half for a wagon train. Another point of interest is the three-state corner eight miles west of Elkhart. Kansas, Oklahoma, and Colorado intersect here.

There is a spirit in this town, this county, that goes beyond surviving. This spirit goes on to win. Significantly, Elkhart is the smallest town in the United States to host a Summer Collegiate Baseball team, but their Elkhart Dusters placed fifth in the National Baseball Congress World Series in 1994.

The place where Kansas, Oklahoma, and Colorado intersect

Ellsworth
Cowboys Are Real

There is resonance in the morning mists of Ellsworth County. It remembers the cataclysmic time when the hills were born, recalls the hand that carved the petroglyphs, resurrects the unruly Texas cowboy... and speaks eloquently of Ellsworth today. The past created Ellsworth, and the past seems tangible here.

There is a place south of Ellsworth where for millenia thousands of buffalo plunged and slipped down a rocky cliff to reach the water in Ash Creek. Hidden by vegetation and only fifty feet from a highway, clear, distinct tracks carved by millions of hooves remain. The last buffalo to descend may have heard the locomotive whistle in 1867 that sealed its fate.

Little Mushroom State Park with its Alice-in-Wonderland toadstool rock formations lies hidden in a valley. Relax in the shade here and contemplate nature's processes. Wonder, if you will, what forces sculpted these surrealistic formations—rain, frost, wind—and think of the time it must have taken.

Petroglyphs carved in Ellsworth County sandstone by ancient tribes speak with symbols we may not understand. Even though they are written in stone, the elements and the hand of man threaten them. Some are sacred; some tell of the white men coming.

A notable mound, now known as Fremont's Knob, celebrates Captain John C. Fremont's conciliatory speech made here in July of 1844 to Native Americans. The hill is still here, but the promised peace quickly vanished.

Faint depressions in a Smoky Hill River flood plain embankment are evidence of Fort Ellsworth, established in 1864 to protect the frontier from "savages." Soldiers were for a time quartered in riverbank dugouts. The fort was soon renamed Fort Harker and moved to present day Kanopolis, where the old guardhouse serves as a museum and three other original buildings are private residences. The buildings can be identified by their red-brown sandstone exteriors.

Two main streets (parallel, with railroad tracks between, and now mostly vacant) are subtle evidence of Ellsworth's railroad-terminus and cattle-drive-destination days from 1867 to 1875. In that brief period Ellsworth epitomized the American wild frontier. As the cowboy saga was played out, the main streets bristled with saloons, gambling joints, and brothels in between. Buffalo Bill Cody, Wild Bill Hickock, Wyatt

Unusual rock formations in Mushroom State Park

Earp, Doc Holiday, Bat Masterson, and many more dubious heroes of the frontier made their marks in Ellsworth, though little remains to recall their heyday.

But proof cut in stone in a very strange cemetery verifies that the stuff legends are made of is real. A tombstone bearing the name of Chauncey Whitney and dated August 18, 1873, brings to mind one Sunday afternoon long ago when violence exploded in Ellsworth and Sheriff Whitney was gunned down. The Ellsworth police department (Union Civil War veterans referred to as four Jacks and a Joker) refought the war with Texas cattle-drive cowboys (ex-Confederate soldiers), and the sheriff was caught in the middle as a peacemaker.

Graves in Circle Cemetery radiate from a midpoint like spokes on a wheel instead of being set in the traditional east-west orientation. Incidentally, Colonel Henry Inman, namesake of Lake Inman and of my home town, was buried here in 1899.

I become very introspective when I feel the beauty and sense the soul of a place. Sometimes I just walk or drive as if by instinct, but for an area as vast and diverse as Ellsworth County I needed a guide. Jim Gray loves the land, treasures its history, and likes to share his knowledge.

You may find Jim at the Drovers Mercantile on Douglas Street. The store is a step back into cowtown history. The front room is finished out as a cowboy bunkhouse, and in the next room a chuck wagon with all the accoutrements is the centerpiece. The Mercantile focuses on authentic western wear, especially that of the cowtown era.

Jim tells me that as a boy he was a great fan of Gene Autry and Roy Rogers and wanted to be where the real cowboys were when he grew up. He didn't realize then that the real cowboys lived in Ellsworth County and that a good part of the cowboy legend originated in Ellsworth, Kansas.

A wonderful way to experience Ellsworth County is to follow the Kanopolis Lake Legacy Trail, a self-guided automobile tour with good information readily at hand. The total distance is seventy-five miles, but you can pick and choose points of interest.

Whatever you do, allow yourself a half-day to explore the pretty little town of Wilson, the Czech capital of Kansas. I warn you, you may wonder whether you have lost your way and arrived in another country. You'll see bright, colorful banners displayed and store-front signs with foreign-language words, and you'll find kolaches on the restaurant menus (try them, you'll like them).

Most Wilson buildings are made of stone, the trim painted in pastel colors. Dates on the entablatures read 1888, 1889, 1901.... The town is proud of its restored opera house and the House of Memories Museum. A unique round building once served as a water tower on the top level and a jail at the lower level.

Sadly, this beautiful town is suffering economically. Many of these wonderful buildings, including the opera house, are unoccupied most of the time. The opera house dance floor, once a community focal point, now waits silently for the annual After Harvest Czech Festival when the town comes alive again.

Today in Ellsworth, while the main streets sleep, Douglas Street (a very fine thoroughfare on K-14) has become the heart of the business district. Ellsworth streets are safe and secure; cowboys come into town on four-wheelers taking the kids to swimming lessons; they say the hardware store carries anything you might need; and pigeons coo in the old building with the cupola hanging on its side. The motel here looks great to me, especially the indoor pool, and as far as food is concerned you have a choice of ten restaurants.

Come out to Ellsworth. Bring the kids, even the grandkids. Discover for yourself the resonance in the morning mists of Ellsworth County.

Emporia

Front Porch to the Flint Hills

Emporia, "the Front Porch to the Flint Hills": what a curious slogan, I thought.

Jean-Ellen Jantzen, director of Emporia's Visitors Bureau, explained. "If we called Emporia the gateway to the Flint Hills, it would imply you're just passing through town. We invite people to enjoy our hospitality—food, lodging, zoo, and parks—to sit a spell on our front porch after a long day of discovery."

I took her advice; I found my front porch and set out to enjoy the countryside. The Flint Hills were blooming and I was in a hurry to get there, but on my way out of town my eye caught a glimpse of Stonehenge—eight great carved stones set on end—faces, symbols, abstractions. Prairie Passages is the name of this stone congregation, but what was it saying? I pondered the question a while; it stirred my mind, but the answer eluded me. Let me know what you think.

As I drove west to Strong City, the drama of the hills enveloped me—the grand design of the terrain, the deep creeks, silence broken only by a quail calling. I saw them as a work of art on an infinite scale. Suddenly my question grew exponentially: "Why is the beauty of the Flint Hills there? Why not only flat, efficient plains everywhere? What are the hills saying to us?"

I stopped on a remote roadside to listen to the message of the hills. A red-headed woodpecker on a fence post seemed to be doing the same thing. A spider wort caught my eye. I took my close-up camera and zeroed in on it. It was as if all the beauty of the hills was wrapped up in this delicate flower. The detail was awesome—soft blue petals with an iridescent dew drop clinging, six fragile filaments capped with fuzzy yellow anthers, slender veined leaves—all sharp and crystal clear.

Here was nature's perfection only ten feet from the road, but there was more: a colony of wild prairie roses presenting their blushing faces, a spread of purple poppy mallows, clumps of bright orange butterfly milkweed, catclaw sensitive briar shrinking from my touch, and much more, bounty too copious to mention here.

Bedazzled by detail I looked up, and there were the hills, their features so massive that I almost missed them enshrouded in a blue haze. Distances were accentuated by the ethereal curtain, and a stream of sunlight captured cattle on a ridge. A nearby creek gurgled for attention; a little dickcissel

Prairie Passage, a series of sculpted stone pylons

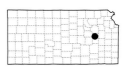

Fishing Bridge across the Cottonwood River

rasped out its song, and a red-wing blackbird warned me that I was in its territory.

No trip to the Flint Hills is complete these days without a stop at the famed and controversial Z-Bar/Spring Hill Ranch (some ranchers question the propriety of it becoming a national park). The land-baron era, a time when individuals carved out vast empires in seemingly unlimited western frontier space, comes to mind when you visit here. The stately mansion, a great stone barn, and other outbuildings will be open to visitors by appointment in 1996. Rumor has it that an underground passage runs from house to barn. I enjoyed the hiking trail; it offered an intimate connection with open range land.

It was time to get back to Emporia, to relax on the front porch. Emporia, of course, was the home of William Allen White, whose editorial prowess elevated him to national and international influence at the turn of the century. I wondered what this great man would think and say now if he were sitting on

this metaphorical front porch. I wondered if the grandeur of the Flint Hills had anything to do with molding his philosophy. Surprisingly, readily available information about White is sparse in Emporia. I would like to know more of him.

Emporia is a healthy, bustling town if traffic is an indicator. Food and lodging abound with a broad range of price and comfort. While it is the ideal home base for Flint Hills excursions, Emporia has its own attractions too, most of them wonderful for children.

Emporia's Municipal Zoo in Soden's Grove appeals to young and old. I tend to be a bit blasé about animals and birds in a zoo after experiencing the Flint Hills and Maxwell Wildlife Refuge, but I must admit it's nice to see more than a fleeting glimpse of a bobcat, a badger, and a deer. This is a happy zoo, the animals are well cared for, it's neat and clean, and as a result people are happy to be there. Prairie dogs and ducks are always fun to watch. Your kids will like rides on the miniature train on summer evenings.

Just across the street from the zoo is something I call basic Americana, the Fishing Bridge over the Cottonwood River. What a pretty sight—anglers of all ages with fishing poles reaching out for that Big One. This beautiful double-arch Marsh bridge was abandoned but wisely preserved when the highway was moved. Peter Pan Park nearby also has fishing spots, shaded picnic areas, and playground equipment.

A bronze sculpture, *Just a Taste,* near the Lyon County Historical Museum is so realistic it fools me every time at first glance. It's a touching scene of a little boy offering a little girl just a taste of his ice cream cone. The ice cream almost melts on a hot day. Real children (and adults too) enjoy the museum's displays and programs that connect Emporia with its roots.

Another bit of nostalgia is a one-room school moved stone by stone to the Emporia State University campus. Built in 1873, this schoolhouse features a coal stove and desks like those in my grade school, the kind the teacher adjusted to the student's size every year with a big wrench.

"Sit a spell" on Emporia's front porch. Reflect on the everlasting hills, the ancient streams, the array of flowers and birds, and the sunset. Ask yourself, "Why are they there?"

Fort Scott

Dolly the Trolley and Painted Ladies

The city of Fort Scott is one big time machine. Pick a date sometime after the 1840s and the time wizards in Fort Scott can introduce you to captains of industry, generals of the army, and the high society of the city's golden days. You can see, you can walk into, you can dine in, and you can sleep in the grand homes of early entrepreneurs. The nice part about it all is that the realism stops just short of bringing back the dusty streets, bad water, and runaway horses.

How can this be? How can you meet Captain Benjamin Moore, the fort's first commander; watch the dragoons drilling; or dine with the early mayor of the town? Well, before we meet these people, we need to know a few things about the town.

Old Fort Scott, the city's namesake, is still there, right in the center of town on a bluff overlooking the Marmaton River. The restoration and reconstruction are so well done it's hard to believe the fort was built in 1842. At that time a line drawn north and south from Fort Scott was considered the permanent Indian frontier.

The first year two companies of dragoons (elite frontier troops trained to fight on foot or horseback) were stationed here. The fort was closed in 1853, but the army returned for a time during the Civil War.

During the summer many events and re-enactors bring back the fort's daily routine of the 1840s. In September you can meet the dragoons during Mexican War Encampment. About seventy-five thousand people visit here annually.

It doesn't take long to realize that Fort Scott is an old town by Kansas standards. The frontier military road running from Fort Leavenworth to Fort Gibson in Oklahoma was built in the late 1830s. Early Fort Scott played a vital role in protecting the rights of Indian tribes west of the military road and in the war with Mexico.

From a Main Street vantage point you can still see the old fort and commercial buildings constructed before the Civil War. It's possible that Osage Indians, free-state and slave-state advocates, and army dragoons mingled in these structures. Several retail establishments bear an 1863 date on the front facades.

Dolly the Trolley is part of

The visitor center at the Fort Scott National Historic Site

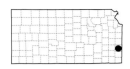

Main Street buildings in Fort Scott reflect late 1800s charm

the Fort Scott time machine. You sit down on one of her benches, and, if her transmission is working (it balked the first day I was there), early Kansas history begins to unfurl before you. A very eloquent guide narrates, pointing out what even my new explorer eyes might have missed. I certainly would have overlooked the ornate painted ladies—colorful Victorian homes restored to their original elegance. Then there are the houses purchased from the Sears Roebuck catalog and shipped out in crates. The price of one assembled in 1910 was $210.

Our trolley tour stopped off at the National Cemetery, and I learned that it was the first of twelve National Cemeteries established by President Lincoln (Arlington National Cemetery is number two). Confederate soldiers are buried here also but at an oblique angle. Sixteen Native American Civil War veterans rest here. The black soldiers known as Buffalo Soldiers are represented as well; their graves are distinguished by tombstones that are shorter than the others.

Other things I learned on the trolley ride: Gordon Parks was born in Fort Scott and his film *The Learning Tree* was based on events here; Fort Scott has thirty miles of brick streets; and old vintage houses had stepping stones

at the curbs so ladies could exit their carriages gracefully.

Back to the time machine and Main Street. The old and new do mix well here. The turn-of-the-century charm, bright colors, and ornate detail of old Main Street have been retained, but discreet adaptations make the buildings remarkably functional as retail shops. Art, antique, gift, and craft shops share frontage space with upscale clothing stores and modern merchandise and service facilities.

Charles and Kathryn Reed's Corner of Time antiques and collectibles store is indeed one reminder of a corner of a time that was. Kathryn loves to talk about old Fort Scott as well as marketing bits and pieces of the past.

Another enthusiastic promoter of downtown Fort Scott is Judy Renard. In her circa 1895 old-fashioned country store she sells nostalgic and Victorian gifts and reproductions and

hand-crafted items. Judy explained that the restoration of Fort Scott's Victorian downtown was a cooperative effort. She and the Reeds represent many fine merchants that have maintained this Victorian treasure for us.

Did you think bib overalls had gone out with the pitchfork? Key Industries of Fort Scott ships new overalls out by the hundreds of thousands annually. You'll find their retail outlet in a beautifully restored shop on Main Street, where you'll discover not only overalls but a wide selection of contemporary work and casual clothes.

Not only does the Fort Scott time machine take you back to things and places of the past, it lets you luxuriate for a short time in the opulence only the rich experienced in early Fort Scott. A special event, An Evening of Victorian Elegance, is hosted by Pat Lyons of Lyons House. She recreates social events described in 1890s society columns for groups of up to thirty-four. The party is a nine-course feast on tables set with fine linens, silver, china, and crystal. Special guests (actors portraying 1890s dignitaries), entertainers, and servers are all dressed in period costumes. A number of Victorian bed-and-breakfasts welcome you for the night. Why not live like an aristocrat for a day or two in Fort Scott?

Fredonia
Moonlight on the Old Millstream

Fredonia nestles in the Fall River Valley between two primeval hillocks. A sense of anticipation was building as I drove into town, but no billboards or flashing marquees accosted me.

It seemed logical to begin my Fredonia exploration at the area's high point, South Mound. From this lofty vantage place, a canopy of trees veiled the town several hundred feet below. Only a few landmarks were clearly visible: the city square with its clock tower and the Gold Dust Hotel; grain elevators; the green and red of the beautiful new high school and athletic complex, where the prestigious Fredonia Relays are held; and South Mound's twin a mile to the west. South Mound is a good place to picnic, with shelters for shade and playground equipment for the kids.

The romantic spirit in me loved Fredonia's old mill dam. As I watched, its cool water rushing over the dam seemed to wash my worldly cares away. Shallow water splashed and played in Fall River's rocky bed, glistening in moonlight. If the water is low enough, you may cross the low-water bridge across the river with your car. This setting may someday be discovered by Hollywood, but for now it is a genuine Kansas treasure.

Along the road leading to the old mill are picturesque limestone ruins of a 1910-1920s-era gasoline refinery. Early this century oil and gas discoveries led to a boom in the area. Enterprises such as zinc smelters and glass, brick, and cement factories flourished briefly. Today only cement plants and some oil activity remain.

For excitement explore the Fall River on a five-mile canoe trip from the old mill to Oxbow Bend near the Rocky Ridge Resort. This delightful resort offers fine dining, lodging, and R.V. hook-ups. Kids will love the pygmy goats, the llamas, the zebus, and the swimming pool. Owners Jack and Mary Jo describe the restaurant decor as "early Kansas." The salad bar is an old Model T truck, and the view from the large windows overlooking the Oxbow Bend is Kansas at its natural best. The Rocky Ridge Resort is a wonderful place for retreats and reunions. Of course, you can reach it by road as well as by river.

Fredonia seems to have a flair for the unusual. The Wilson County Museum is housed in the old jail. The heavy barred doors are still there. In fact, the curator recalled a man visiting with his son and showing him his former cell. Really, can you feature a spinning wheel, a parasol, and baby clothes in a jail cell?

The Fredonia Arts Council is housed in the "Stone House," the oldest house in town, circa 1872. It's on the Kansas State Historic Register. The juried national art exhibits on display are a good reason to step in and enjoy the art. And be sure to check out the house. You'll probably say, "They don't build them like they used to any more."

On the north side of the city square a large mechanical clock, once atop the old courthouse, now stands and strikes the hour. The face, high on a tower, is operated by remote control. It's interesting to watch the clock works through large windows at street level, and kids (including me) love to see the gears and fans whirring when the clock strikes.

Exotic animals wander the grounds at Rocky Ridge Resort

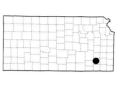

The old mill on the Fall River near Fredonia

East of the city square the Gold Dust Hotel, built in 1885, now houses the Chamber of Commerce and the Gold Dust Salon. Inquire at the Chamber office for detailed Fredonia information. As you walk in try to imagine the hustle and bustle of the oil-boom years. Picture the "important" financiers, the oil speculators, and the rough-and-tumble drillers right where you are now. Envision people dressed in high style mingling and laughing, in a festive mood. Then go outside and look at the forlorn windows of the upper stories. Can't you almost see them cry?

For a change of pace I went to the Friend Exotic Bird Farm and Antiques. Birds of all colors dazzled me, and the antiques brought back memories (almost made *me* feel like an antique). This is a working bird farm, so please see J.W. or Keri before

you wander around. The splendor of peacocks strutting their stuff, especially the pure white ones, and the exotic pheasants, ducks, turkeys, and more decked in their brilliant plumage are a celebration of color.

"Come shoot with us" is the invitation from Elkhorn Sporting Clays northwest of Fredonia. What better place to enjoy the sport than in this Chautauqua Hills woodland of black jack and white oaks. In 1994 they hosted the Zone 6 National Sporting Clays Championships. For the casual traveler there is opportunity to see Sitka deer, Dubaski deer (a Russian variety), fallow deer, and Rocky Mountain elk wandering in the woodlands as you pass by on the scenic public roads.

Hunting is great in the Fredonia area. White-tail deer, turkey, and quail abound, but most of the immediate-area hunting is

on private land. You must make contact with owners for permission. The Kansas Department of Wildlife and Parks offers great public hunting sites within thirty minutes of Fredonia.

West of Fredonia in the Chautauqua Hills and north of town along the Verdigris River Valley, country roads are an off-the-blue-highways explorer's delight. Roads become fascinating byways, meandering through woodlands, meadows, and fields. You'll find oil-boom-era ruins, now quaint relics. There are rustic farms, low-water bridges, and fence posts resembling stone cairns.

Just as in Fredonia's Stone House art displays, the landscape's grandeur is constantly renewed by the grand curator of the hills and river valleys. In season, wildflowers and avian flowers—dazzling goldfinches, scissor-tailed flycatchers, yellow-headed blackbirds—change the scene every day. Fertile black soil in winter repose yields green blades of corn and milo that mature to harvest gold.

Journey to Benedict, Coyville, and New Albany. Hide your cellular phone, imagine yourself in a DeSoto or Studebaker, and the computer age will vanish. Approach these villages with love and compassion and listen to their voices. Back in Fredonia you'll find fine food and a good night's rest.

Harper County
Gateway to the Wild and Wicked West

I need your help! Exploring Harper County is too much for one person. The people of Harper County are too busy living normal, prosperous lives to fuss about their visitor attractions and advantages. They are rather embarrassed that they don't have any snow-capped mountains or sandy beaches, but they just love things as they are. No fancy brochures hype up the allure of Harper County. Citizens say they know who they are and where they're going.

Indeed, nobody gets excited about something like the Crisfield diamond mines. In fact, nobody seems to remember where Crisfield is. Rumor has it that they weren't the best-quality diamonds anyway, and they wouldn't have provided much employment. The diamonds reportedly lay on the surface and wouldn't have required much labor to mine.

In the olden days the Ninety-Eighth Meridian just east of Harper was considered "the Gateway to the Wild Wicked West." I even saw an almost-forgotten proposal to build an arch over U.S. Highway 160 welcoming travelers to the Wild West. Apparently the good people of Harper don't feel this claim is justified. Machine Gun Kelly and Pretty Boy Floyd were said to have passed through the area in the thirties. Actually, U.S. 160, the southern route across Kansas, is one of the state's most scenic roads. Somewhere between Danville and Harper, U.S. 160 crosses the boundary between rich wheat land in eastern Harper County and the famed Red Hills of south central Kansas.

From a distance, especially from the west, Danville is a very picturesque town, with a gleaming white church spire backgrounded by white grain elevators and overlooking a tree-shaded village. Closer inspection reveals the decay familiar in many small towns. As farms grow larger the economic base of small-community services—grocery, hardware, and clothing stores—decreases, and businesses fade away. At one time Danville was one of the largest Harley-Davidson distribution points in the country. The only evidence remaining is a large concrete slab and, they say, the frameworks of many houses constructed with motorcycle packing crates.

Freeport, population 10, is the smallest incorporated town in the U.S.A. Carol Peterson, the postmistress, presides over sixteen city mailboxes and the rural route. She has a lot of stories to tell about Freeport and loves doing so. In 1885 the town had two names, Freeport and Midlothian. To resolve the issue a fence was set down the middle of Grand Avenue, dividing the town, but "Freeport" eventually won out. Briefly, just before the Cherokee Outlet Run, Freeport had a population of five hundred. Precisely at noon on September 13, 1893, almost everyone left Freeport, never to return.

Harper County has seen fancy ideas come and go. In the 1890s an Irish promoter convinced dukes and lords in England that Kansas was the place to train their playful sons in the art of farming. So, also briefly, Runnymede became home to a hundred "remittance men." To facilitate their quest for agrarian knowledge they built a fine hotel, polo grounds, a race track, a steeplechase course, and other things needed to make life on the plains tolerable. Can you imagine the sight of mounted red-coated hunters and baying hounds pursuing a lowly coyote, or a tallyho stagecoach on its way to Harper with a band on top serenading the passengers within?

Today a wheat field covers the memories, and the only tangible

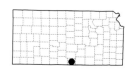

English "Remittance Men" built the Runnymede Church

restaurant with menu items ranging from apple pie to Tex-Mex. A bit further down the road is Jo's Place, where farmers go for breakfast and ladies have coffee hour at their own round table. On the same street the Country Blessings Gift Shop (some call it a "darling" little shop) sells gifts, antiques, and the finest homemade gourmet fudge imaginable.

Anthony, the county seat, has the oldest pari-mutuel horse-racing track in Kansas. Begun in 1904, races have been run annually ever since in July. In 1940 dog racing was added to the schedule. The venerable grandstand is worth a stop anytime. At the courthouse, aficionados will see similarities to other county courthouses also designed by G. H. Washburn. One of the few remaining drive-in theaters in Kansas is slated to reopen for the 1996 summer season north of Anthony. Don't let the imposing fence keep you from enjoying the Anthony Historical Museum in the classic brick Santa Fe depot.

The elements of rural culture may not jump at you in Harper County, but the patient Kansas explorer searching with new eyes will be well rewarded. Lodging and restaurants are good in both towns. Incidentally, Harper is the only town I've ever seen with a huge fish weather vane on top of its water tower.

reminder, the Runnymede Church, has been moved to Harper. The rather plain exterior belies the ornate interior, which includes a stone baptismal font imported from England. Not far from the old Runnymede Church is a delightful park and playground children love.

How do you find something when it isn't there? I kept hearing about the Main Street fountain in Harper, but I couldn't

The Harper County Courthouse in Anthony

find it. Gail Bellar from the Harper Museum finally explained it to me. The fountain is not a fountain; it's a cluster of lights on an elegant pedestal at the main intersection. Originally a horse-watering trough was located here. As its relevance diminished, an elaborate fountain was installed, but the designer of the fountain forgot about the Kansas winds; water sprayed all over town. So lights replaced the water, but everyone still speaks of the fountain.

North of the fountain is a colorful mural leading to a street with a number of nice gift shops. Sue's Country Closet sells unusual yard ornaments—Santa, a snowman, toy soldiers at Christmastime, witches and goblins for Halloween, and others for summertime—all in bright colors.

A few blocks south on the highway is the Country Creamery in an old Standard filling station. It's actually a snug

Hiawatha
A Windmill Garden

Hiawatha, City of Beautiful Maples. These are such wonderful trees. In summer their green canopy cools and refreshes the lawns and walkways below, and in the fall their glorious reds warm the heart as winter nears. October's miracle of changing colors is indeed a sight to behold in Hiawatha. Children play; some people run, some walk, and lovers stroll arm in arm basking in the pleasure of it all.

Then there are the windmills—windmill after windmill reaching to the sky like spring flowers, always turning their faces into the wind. Don Quixote would have had a fearsome time dueling with the windmills of Hiawatha. (How do you describe a large number of windmills? Do you say a "covey" of windmills, or a "herd," or a "gaggle"?) Anyway, this "multitude" of windmills greeted me when I walked out of the Hiawatha Heartland Inn after breakfast. Their shimmering sil-

ver fans take up nearly the whole eastern horizon. It was something I couldn't resist exploring.

Of all things man-made, I can think of nothing that comes closer to being natural than a windmill. It's outside, it reaches to the sky for energy, and it reaches down into the earth for precious water. A windmill uses natural energy, and its withdrawal of earth's resources is always modest.

The Ag Museum complex associated with the windmills takes you back to grandpa's farm. A ten-by-twenty-foot display, artistically crafted, recalls a time when farms were more diversified. The early 1900s farmstead features a farmhouse, a barn, a hog house, an open implement shed, a henhouse, corrals, and even a privy. Larger exhibits include old tractors, cars, and farm machinery.

Outside I met Leon Wenger, a spry eighty-one years old, repairing an old corn crib just moved to the site. We found we

had many interests in common, and we discussed how few people even recognize a corn crib or a hayrack for what they were. He recalled how he and friends were talking about the number of dairy farms closing and speculating where milk would eventually be coming from. A young lady popped up with the comment, "Don't worry; the grocery stores always have milk."

With misty eyes Leon continued, "I want my grandchildren to know how it used to be on the farm and where food comes from."

Ernie's Workshop located on the premises is a novel concept more communities may want to copy. Senior citizens may use the facilities for craft projects, which are sold in the museum gift shop. The shop also provided working space for museum construction projects.

Across the road you'll discover a mystery cast in Italian marble. More than twenty thousand people visit Hiawatha's Mt. Hope Cemetery every year to see the Davis Memorial. A fifty-two-ton marble canopy set on stone pillars caps eleven life-size Italian marble statues depicting various stages in the married life of John and Sarah Davis. Having lived frugally on a farm near Hiawatha, John Davis surprised the whole community when upon Sarah's death in 1930 he commissioned a most lavish memorial. Stories as to where the

Leon Wenger repairing a corn crib

A windmill in Hiawatha's Windmill Garden

money came from and why he neglected local charities abound. One version is that her parents deemed him unworthy of her and specified in their will that the only part of their fortune John could ever inherit must be spent on Sarah's memorial. A vacant marble chair next to an aging statue of John depicts his last years alone. See it to believe it.

The Memorial Auditorium in Hiawatha, now the Brown County Museum, evokes more nostalgia. The old front porch with its fancy wood trim and porch swing for two will bring back romantic memories for many, I'm sure. In this spacious museum entire rooms of period homes and businesses are recreated. Featured are the old Robinson Pharmacy complete with soda fountain, a Western Union office, a baby's room, and a general store, to mention just a few.

Main Street in Hiawatha is an avenue of maple trees leading to the courthouse square and downtown. The Old Town Clock high up in its round turret gives the town a Byzantine fla-

vor. Nearby some very fine gift shops (that would probably be called "boutiques" in an urban setting) are a visitor's mecca.

I visited Bonnie's Jewelry and Gifts and was glad to see displayed—along with the Hummels, Cherished Teddies, Mary's Moo Moos, cut glass, and fine jewelry—a Kansas Corner including our own Kansas guidebooks. Bonnie Howard has every right to be proud of her shop, but very graciously she introduced me to two adjoining gift shops, Carol's Hallmark and the Alligator Gift Shop and Tea

Hiawatha is noted for its beautiful maple trees

Room. The Alligator's menu board reads, "Our menu is low fat, but our desserts are the sinful exception."

In town and out on blacktop roads it's hard to visualize the lone Pony Express rider of pre-Civil War days racing his horse over the prairie. At Kennekuk, south of Horton, memories of the Pony Express, stagecoaches, and freight wagons still seem to linger in the hills. Maybe it's because the modern world has not overwhelmed the land here. An abandoned store, falling apart, marks the area where once two hotels, a livery stable, general stores, and churches catered to travelers. A sign and monument commemorate the Pony Express.

Browsing through the county around Hiawatha I marveled at the rich black earth turned up by plows. The modern farm tractors and implements here bear little resemblance to those I saw in the Ag Museum, but some where between Everest and Willis I found a farmstead with a henhouse, a brooder house, a barn with vertical siding, and a privy. With regret I observed that the mom-and-pop grocery store at Willis had closed its doors. For local rural ambience try the cafes at Fairview and Everest for breakfast or lunch.

You'll have a good time in Hiawatha and Brown County, and your faith in America will be renewed.

Hillsboro

A Dutch Treat

For a Dutch treat, Hillsboro is the place to go. If you're not acquainted with the Dutch cuisine, you'll love verenika, German smoked sausage, fried potatoes, rich gravy, zwieback, and peppernuts.

Hillsboro, of course, is not exclusively of Dutch origin, but the Dutch imprint is here—a Dutch mill, Dutch food, a nearly lost unwritten Dutch dialect, and the Dutch Mennonite Pioneer Museum. Some say the word "Dutch" is incorrect, pointing out that the Mennonite immigrants were actually Russian or German. The truth is they fled religious persecuton in Holland during the 1500s and over a three-hundred-year period emigrated to Prussia, Russia, and finally the United States.

Whatever word you use, the people of Hillsboro exemplify the virtues of hard work, thrift, and cleanliness in this friendly, thriving city. Prosperous farms, a growing manufacturing complex, a hospital, an excellent school system, and a college provide a strong economic base. Downtown are the traditional full-service stores—grocery, clothing, furniture, hardware, lumber, and—very unusual in a town of twenty-seven hundred—three automobile dealers.

The past is important to Hillsboro. The house built in 1909 by William and Ida Schaeffler, German Lutheran immigrants, has been carefully restored to offer a glimpse of life in the early part of this century. One room interprets Hillsboro business history and another features Hillsboro pioneers. I see the fine woodwork, stained-glass windows, and—an extra touch—a round cupola as expressions of faith in a dynamic quality of life for years to come.

Walk into the Pioneer Adobe Museum and pretend you're visiting your great-great-grandparents' farm in 1879. Keep in mind that when these pioneers arrived only five years earlier the area was a sea of grass and population was very sparse. They plowed up the sod and planted the precious Turkey Red wheat they had brought from Russia. Building materials were scarce; many built adobe houses made of earth and straw. You'll be surprised at how nice and quiet it is inside. If David Wiebe is your guide, ask him to say the names of the rooms in the Low Dutch vernacular— *klena shtov, feashtov,* and the *keack* (hint: *shtov* means "room"). The clock you see on the wall may have been one of the few precious possessions brought in a trunk from Russia. Imagine big loaves of rye bread and zwieback baking in the large straw-fired stove built into the inner walls of the house.

Open the north door and—surprise!—you're in the barn. What could be more cozy than family and animals under the same roof on a cold winter day when the snow is blowing across miles of open prairie? In this case the barn, added a few years after the house was built, was made of lumber. Here in the Pioneer Museum the ani-

The replicated and functional Friesen Dutch mill

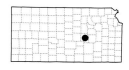

The Adobe House Museum in Hillsboro

mals have been replaced with the tools and crude implements farmers used in that early time. Threshing stones, like the one displayed here, were used only for a few years in America before mechanical threshers replaced them.

Continue your make-believe 1879 visit as you clamber up a ladder into the Friesen Dutch Mill, a full-size replica of a wind-powered grist mill built by Jacob Friesen in 1876. Wagonloads of wheat were brought here to to be ground into flour. The grain was carried up to the grinding level, and soon the huge ponderous wheel would catch the wind and begin to turn. Massive wooden gears growl as they mesh, and the whole building vibrates as the millstones crush the corn.

Only one photograph of the original mill existed to guide millwright Richard Wall, a Tabor College biology professor, in the design of the replica. A barn built by Jacob Friesen and still standing offered insight as to frame and joinery details and the use of square nails.

On an empty hill a mile and a

half south of Hillsboro, where once the village of Gnadenau flourished, a simple epitaph on a stone reads, "In memory of Krimmer Mennonite Brethren." The *Marion County Record* reported in December 1875, "Gnadenau is a quaint little Mennonite town of 100 or 150.... Homes are built in Russian style with family and livestock all under one roof.... Gnadenau presented a picturesque appearance... in its wealth of beautiful flowers, which appeared as immense bouquets." It's all gone now; only the forlorn Jacob Friesen barn remains.

Getting back to the smoked sausage.... Hillsboro prides itself as being the smoked-sausage capital of North America. In May the town hosts a smoked-sausage festival. There are sausage sandwiches, a sausage cookoff, sausage cooking demos, a butchering museum, music—gospel, bluegrass, and country—plus a family-style sausage supper. Just breathing the air cranks up the taste buds as sausage is consumed by the ton. Then in September one of the

most colossal arts-and-crafts fairs in Kansas draws more than thirty thousand people to view and purchase fine works produced by regional and nationally known artisans and craftsmen.

There's a special place in Hillsboro that incorporates almost all the rural culture elements—the 1887 Old Towne. This fine restaurant features the best of Hillsboro Dutch cuisine as well as American and south-of-the-border entrees. A 1940s soda fountain stands out as "modern" in this native limestone building, which at one time was a processing center for millions of eggs, chickens, pigeons, quail, and rabbits. Eggs were candled in what is now the main dining room, and the Southwest dining room was a walk-in cooler holding four thousand cases of eggs. Old Towne is the place to meet Hillsboro's business leaders.

For authentic Low Dutch conversation or folk stories, talk to Irv Schroeder at his auto agency. You'll soon see the humor inherent in this colloquial dialect. Even people who can't understand a word of Low Dutch find his Will Rogers–style monologues hilarious. In fact, he does radio commercials in Low Dutch, and people come to his store just to see what he said.

Hillsboro is a lovely city and an ethnic treat. Make it part of your Kansas exploration.

Inman

My Hometown

Inman, my hometown. What do you say about a place you know so well that everything seems commonplace? I find myself thinking the thoughts expressed by citizens of many towns when I ask them, "What is special about your town?"

*The answer usually is something like, "I really can't think of anything special here in our town. We're here, going about our daily living and work, just ordinary folk." But the truth of the matter is, it's the simple words—*here, living, work, *and* ordinary folk*—that create the drama of life anywhere.*

The hill later called Inman was always *here*. For a long time it was covered with grasses bending under prairie winds, visited by herds of buffalo and people we call Native Americans. To the east was a valley of shallow lakes teeming with waterfowl, and to the west on the horizon could be seen from time to time roiling clouds of sand forming the dunes now called sand hills.

During the Indian War days, Colonel Henry Inman, maybe in the company of his friend Buffalo Bill Cody, noted in his journal a large lake in McPherson County that consequently was named for him. With later arrivals on this hill—settlers, predominantly Russian Mennonites and German Evangelicals; the Rock Island Railroad; and the United States post office—pristine geography yielded to civilization, and history took a dramatic turn as a town named after a nearby lake sprang to life.

The architecture of early Inman (originally Aiken) was western "hurry-up" wood frame. Indeed, on a chilly day in February 1887, two men raced on a wagon to Conway for lumber to build the first store in Inman, and when they returned they found that another gentleman had dragged his blacksmith shop from nearby Farland into the new town. Rumor has it that this early store, in spite of the hurry, endured almost a hundred years until this author's bulldozer ran over it.

What the people of early Inman built reflected their faith in God, in their own hands, and in future generations. They built schools, churches, farm homes, and barns before they built the town. An outstanding Stan Herd mural depicting Inman at the turn of the century shows buildings that are still in use today: the mill, the depot (moved and restored), an Odd Fellows Hall (now a beautifully restored city library), an elevator, and a retail store.

Viewed from inside the nearby bank, the Herd mural appears three dimensional. Its realism captures the entrepreneurial yet pastoral spirit of the pioneer era that even now continues in Inman and so many other rural communities.

Work, not just as a way of making money but as a meaningful part of *living*, is important in Inman. Street conversation in town is not so much about what the government should do for us as what we can do for ourselves, especially if not stifled by unnecessary regulations. Let me illustrate by telling what some of the *ordinary folk* of Inman have accomplished.

It never occurred to Pete

Harold Spencer eating verenika in Ruthie's Cafe

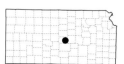

The City of Inman silhouetted by a glorious Kansas sunset

Froese and George Plett to wait for a government assistance program—they created jobs for themselves and many others. Pete invented a self-propelled silage cutter and George helped perfect it. I recall a very cold day, probably in the 1940s; Pete was out alone in a field, hand-feeding sorghum bundles into an experimental machine. He worked on it for years, and as a result, decades later, thirty crews of silage harvesters were operating out of the Inman community. Plett went on to build factory prototypes and some of the first successful self-propelled combines in the country.

There is a family in Inman that has a passion for recycling houses and commercial buildings. Leonard and Louise Friesen, with their children and grandchildren, work in the construction trades and in their spare time renovate buildings—usually three or four at a time. The Friesens target almost any empty building and convert it into a community asset. Granddaughter Darcel and husband Randy moved a huge old farmhouse

into town and are remodeling it as their home. The idea is catching on; Dan and Susan Dirks saved what was a 1930s showplace home from demolition by moving it and restoring it.

Jim and Bonnie Miller are disproving the myth that small-town retailers can't compete with the big cities. By offering fair prices, reliable product information, twenty-one years of experience, and real old-fashioned service, they sell an astonishing amount of household appliances. Ken Froese of rural Inman operates one of the larger pivot irrigation companies in Kansas and sees no small-town disadvantage in serving customers in a one-hundred-mile radius. Goertzen Homes builds houses on site or loads them on trucks and hauls them to any destination within two hundred fifty miles. Many other building contractors, electricians, plumbers, excavators, and craftsmen work out of Inman, a town with a population of just over a thousand.

Agriculture, namely wheat, corn, milo, beans, alfalfa, and

some livestock, is the economic basis of Inman. As larger farms and more efficient farm machinery reduce the farm labor requirement, Inman, like many other small towns, copes by providing services for the new ag economy and for non-agricultural needs.

Stanley Goertzen, a young farmer, saw the handwriting on the wall and acted. He built and designed his own extruder to produce dog food from local milo. Today thousands of tons of local crops are utilized by this plant, now operated by a large corporation.

Inman's McCormick-Deering Days Museum expands on the Stan Herd mural theme by focusing on Inman during the period when the McCormick-Deering tractors and grain binders were state-of-the-art technology. Across the street from the museum, the big stone Odd Fellows hall was a hardware and McCormick-Deering store when I was a youngster; happily I remember the aroma of binder twine and grease and the mysteries of sprockets and chains and cream separators. The museum evokes these memories and many more of one-room school days, the doctor's office, and Model T Fords.

Inman welcomes you; stop in at Ruthie's Cafe (German food on Thursdays) and catch the entrepreneurial vision.

Jefferson County

Passing the Torch

Four fawns and a doe, only 75 yards away! I eased my car to a stop as gently as I could and fumbled for my camera. The light was perfect. . . and I was out of film. The doe raised her head and looked at me and stamped her foot. One fawn pranced about and the others stood there like statues. "Strange," I thought as I hurriedly reloaded; "one doe with three fawns." She was getting restive, snapping her head from side to side. My luck continued. I got off three shots before they bounded into the woods.

The vision of those exuberant little bodies, clearly delineated against green foliage, eyes alert and hearts pure of avarice touched me briefly then but remains clear and crisp in my soul. Driving around the western shore of Lake Perry I had already encountered two flocks of wild turkeys, a skein of geese flying low with their wings almost hitting water, and pelicans in conference near the shore.

Jefferson County is a beautiful place where wooded hills, tracts of farmland, and small towns encircle Lake Perry like a doughnut. Jefferson County is also unique; it offers rare glimpses of Americana such as Apple Valley Farm, the quaint shops of Valley Falls, and a luxurious inn in a barn. Let me whet your exploring appetite by telling you about my discoveries here.

In this rural setting Tom and Marcella Ryan have converted an old barn, built in 1893, into a modern bed-and-breakfast inn. The barn's story is similar to that of the proverbial four hundred-year-old hatchet that had the handle replaced five times and the head three times. In spite of renovations and additions the architectural style and pastoral charm remain. The Barn, as it is called, fits perfectly into the picturesque landscape. Inside, the Ryans share a family atmosphere with thousands of guests a year. They are an excellent source of explorer information.

In nearby Valley Falls (with a population of 1,253, the largest town in the county), I had fascinating conversations with citizens that connected the past and the present. Frank at the pharmacy recalled old-timers talking about Buffalo Bill growing up in Valley Falls. Frank says, "We talk history and UFO's here," and quietly adds, "when we're not busy." Stop in at Frank's Pharmacy for a delightful soda fountain concoction and ask the waitress if you may talk history with Frank.

Down the street I found Helen Stewart, proud of being eighty years old and still sprightly, managing her hardware store. What a store it is. Her sign says, "Fishing spoken here." Like Frank, she sells modern necessities, but still on display are the products the store sold in the 1890s—buggy whip sockets, block planes, wick trimmers, and from a later era a Coleman gasoline iron just like the one my mother used in the thirties. Helen offers the customer value that supermarkets will never attain with their slick discounts.

With a twinkle in her eye

Harold Royer, Valley Falls blacksmith

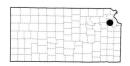

The Barn Bed-and-Breakfast, rural Valley Falls

Helen introduced me to a brawny, bearded gentleman dressed in overalls.

"Mil," she said, "you must see Harold's blacksmith shop." The word "blacksmith" got my attention. I offered to meet him soon.

"No," he said, "you have to follow me."

Away we went down the ancient back streets of Valley Falls, finally ending up in an alley near a nondescript tin shed. Harold pushed through some weeds to unlock a small door. It was dark inside till Harold found a light switch, and there it was, an old-time blacksmith shop: the trip hammer, an anvil, even plowshares on the floor, a forge, and the suspended line shaft driven by a bulky three-phase motor. What memories! Finally, seeing my appreciation, he told me he owned a 1914 Russell steam tractor in parade condition.

Harold was getting on in years too. I wondered how we can ever preserve the experience, knowledge, and human interest that Frank, Helen, and Harold represent.

Minutes later I met a pretty young lady, Laurel Heath, proprietor of the store called Sign of the Times. In her attractive shop are candies, potpourri, bath and herbal products, balloons, and "Land of Kansas" products. I was happy to see her youthful enthusiasm added to the Valley Falls Main Street team.

On the other side of the county I discovered Winchester Hardware, way out in the country. Inside a plain steel building Karen Edmond's fervent energy lit up the store. Her rare and almost naive desire to please customers impressed me. Besides selling hardware and a full line of fabric and sewing notions she teaches machine quilting. In fact she taught husband Charles to make a "broken star" pattern quilt.

You must give in to the gourmet explorer within you to have lunch at Snickerdoodle's across from the courthouse square in Oskaloosa. Carole Hendrix, the owner, says, "Just saying 'Snickerdoodle' brings to mind thoughts of a kitchen warmed with love and laughter and the aroma of sugar and

spice." Enjoy sumptuous salads, sandwiches, connoisseurs' soups, and scrumptious desserts amid gifts, antiques, and unique furniture. After lunch visit Old Jefferson Town, a collection of vintage buildings moved in from Jefferson County locations.

Capturing the enthusiasm Laurel, Karen, and Carole presented, I believed it possible that the Jefferson County spirit might carry on.

To top off your Jefferson County adventures go to Apple Valley Farm for an evening of food, fun, and frivolity. Meredith Day and family have converted this 1850s homestead into a place to enjoy. Dine with gusto in the Farmhouse Restaurant, browse through the Milkbarn arts-and-crafts shop, party in the Granary Saloon, and enjoy the Ric Averill Players melodramas in the Apple Valley Theater. You'll be glad you discovered them, but do call for reservations.

Take time to explore the byways around Lake Perry. If you like water recreation and camping, you'll find marinas, campgrounds, boat ramps, and good fishing too.

Keep it simple, call the Barn for lodging reservations, call Apple Valley Farm for theater reservations (May through September), and fill in the blank spaces with leisurely trips to the little towns and hamlets of Jefferson County.

Kingman

The Gentle Coo of a Mourning Dove

No doubt it was the old Kingman city hall with its castle-like turrets that made me think of Norman Rockwell's home-town America. Main Street's pleasant store fronts and trees and the millstream in Riverside Park are also part of Kingman's timeless charm.

Watching water cascading through the millstream water gates, I imagined one of those rare summer afternoons when a few fluffy white clouds keep the hot sun in check. I would be here holding granddaughters Alyssa and Sofi by the hand, leading them to the nearby playground. I would tell them about a time long ago when a mill, now not even a memory, would grind wheat and corn brought in by horse-drawn wagons.

I'd take the girls to the former Santa Fe depot and I would tell them about the great steam locomotives that rolled through town whistling amid a cloud of trailing smoke. We would walk down Main Street, stopping for a treat at Ken's Deli-Dali while their mothers shopped for antiques and gifts. I'm sure Alyssa, the older of the two girls, would notice the art-deco theater's pretty pastel colors.

Kingman jeweler Lonny Bauer recently told me about some venerable Main Street buildings.

"See the dates on them? Most are pre-1890. You see, a depression hit in 1890 and halted construction all across the nation." These early buildings can be identified by their massive entablatures (decorative tops of the building facades). The early First National Bank building at A and Main is an example of the early style. Compare this with the Romanesque Revival–style Kingman County courthouse, circa 1908.

Of course, I wouldn't bother my little girls with these architectural details, but I would take them to the first Kingman city hall, now the Kingman County Museum. They'd probably think it looked a lot like the Disney Castle. It is a very lovely building, but the tallest turret was at one time functional. When built in 1888 the structure was both city hall and fire department. Early fire hoses required drying to prevent mildew damage, so firehouses had hose-drying towers. This charming anachronism is one of only five remaining in the United States.

Inside the tower, I'm sure Alyssa would gaze up in wonder to the very top, and little Sofi's eyes would be drawn to the bright red Persch fire truck nearby. The old soda fountain on display would spur me to tell the girls "when-I-was-your-age" stories of soda jerks and their delectable concoctions.

Continuing my reverie near the millstream, I imagined bringing the whole family to the Ninnescah Valley Folk Fest and Art Fair in August. I could almost hear the mellow music of acoustic strings floating through the balmy summer night air; I pictured the cozy campfire sing-along that follows.

Memories of old times roll on in Kingman. Four horse and mule auctions every year bring huge draft horses, spirited mules, tack, and all that goes with the time when horse flesh moved the world—buggies, wagons, sulkey plows, cultivators, and horse powers (bet you don't know what those are) to Kingman. If you've never experienced the excitement and tempo of an animal auction, you must come, for this is true Americana. Expect local motels to be filled as buyers come from many states and countries.

Now for a special treat. Would you like to wander through pristine prairie hills, picking sandhill plums, walking barefoot in sandy-bottomed streams or lying in the shade of a giant cottonwood listening to its gentle conversation? Well, you can. In Kingman County's Byron Walker Wildlife Area you can park and

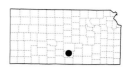

Old wagon at the horse and mule auction in Kingman

roam, if you please, over hill and dale. So relax and sharpen your new explorer eyes to see the fawn in the shadows, the wild turkeys near the woodland edge, and the quietly exquisite wildflowers around you. Breathe the fresh air, feel the spring breeze on your face, hear the gentle coo of a mourning dove, and watch a butterfly floating over the prairie.

If you enjoy a nocturnal chorus of chirpers, bullfrogs, and perhaps the call of a coyote, make camp at nearby Kingman State Fishing Lake. Fish for your supper; they say the crappie and catfish are cooperative. This is a great picnic spot too.

To explore more of rural America head southwest in Kingman County to Zenda, population 96. Some of you will say, as you make the thirty-minute trip down blue highways, "There's nothing to see, it's just miles and miles of loneliness." Others will see productive wheatland and green pastures as well as the strength of the people who farm the fields and call these roads the way to home.

Zenda, nearly empty now, is still full of surprises hidden on the leeward side of the Co-op elevator. Upstairs, in the old city building, turn-of-the-century Zenda is proudly on display, though seen by few. Artist Bonnie Bailey has replicated Zenda in three-dimen-

sional detail. Craft excellence like this should be acclaimed; seeing her work here in this solitary attic is like discovering a diamond in the sand. Another Zenda artist, Edmond Hartshorn, throws and paints delightful ceramics with a local motif.

But that's not all there is in Zenda. You must go to the lumberyard—the Lumberyard Supper Club, that is. What an atmosphere, especially in contrast to your expectations! Many deals for barn lumber once crossed the hostess counter, and the nuts-and-bolts bins are now occupied by the essence of grapes. The menu, of course, features succulent steaks as well as charbroiled specialties and seafood, plus corn dogs, hamburgers, and chicken strips for the kids. Time your Kingman County journey to be here for supper.

After seeing the jail in Cunningham I cut my speed in half and stopped twice at each stop sign. The old 1890s jail could be described as a white concrete vault. Stop to see Cunningham's museum in the circa 1888 Santa Fe depot. Among the local artifacts inside you'll find a hand-powered washing machine invented and manufactured in Cunningham.

Now if the kids insist on pizza, hamburgers, french fries, and ice cream, you'll find it all on U.S. 54 in Kingman.

Lincoln County
Conceived of Post Rock

On a perfect June morning and only a few miles into Lincoln County I pulled over to the side of the road and jotted down these notes: hazy Smoky Hills...lush green, cattle on ridge, wheat turning gold on plain below...a red-wing blazing on a fence post, rustic stone barn in field.

What more can I say, except to add the azure sky and a gentle breeze?

This set the tone for my Lincoln County tour—nothing pretentious, but oh, so authentically real. Lincoln is a town conceived of post rock—courthouse, city hall, Kyne House Museum—all bearing the post rock brown iron-oxide-stripe trademark in every stone.

In fact, Lincoln County is in the heart of the post rock region. Miles and miles of these cumbersome, yet pastoral, sentinels line the roadsides. Post rock quarried by pioneers helped transform a treeless plain into productive farmland by delineating boundaries and fencing in livestock. The unique layer of post rock limestone (about nine inches thick) is near the surface and can be seen in rocky outcrops and roadside cuts.

Duane Vonada and family, near Sylvan Grove, still quarry post rock the old-fashioned way. They offer demonstrations, farm tours, and custom rock craftsmanship. Duane has been known to stop a planter just to tell and reenact the pioneer post rock story to children.

Lincoln County is mystical. Somehow the sunsets highlighting the soft hills and nature tenaciously carving the deep stream beds have given Lincolnians new eyes to see special beauty. Take Marge Lawson, for example. She is a photo artist par excellence. I watched a man study one of her photos. "Beautiful," he said. "Must have been taken in Eng-land, maybe Scotland; it's got that old-country charm." Wrong! It's Sylvan Grove, Kansas.

Marge helped me see the Smoky Hills in a new way. With a faraway look in her eyes she talked of misty hills; nuances of light, shadow, and sky; colors, subtle and dramatic, changing with the seasons; and the wind caressing the grasses.

The story is told of travelers from London touring Kansas, politely saying, "Oh, how nice," to their guide when shown our big cities and their attractions. However, one evening at dusk—the sun low in the west, working wheat combines silhouetted on the western horizon, and dust particles turning the sky red—the visitors got excited. They stayed overnight in Lincoln with Ivona

Stone fence post, yucca, and grasses on rural roadside

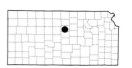

and Michael Pickering, hosts of the Woody House Bed-and-Breakfast. Next morning the Pickerings took the London visitors to Ivona's sister's farm, a fifteen-hundred-acre wheat and cow/calf farm. The large tractors and combines dazzled the Londoners, but it was the simple elegance of asking a blessing before the bounteous harvest noon dinner that was their unforgettable Kansas experience. All stood and held hands as Ivona's brother-in-law offered a prayer of thanksgiving, including the visitors in their circle. It was the genuine experience the visitors had sought.

Marilyn Helmer, owner of Village Lines in Lincoln, also has caught the vision and the desire to share the excitement she feels. Her store is crammed full of Kansas art and crafts, but she'll drop everything to tell you about all the artists and crafters residing in the county. Marilyn says, "The mystique of Lincoln County brings out the art hidden in the soul."

Marilyn is an information clearing house for Lincoln County explorers. She will facilitate everything from a one-hour walking tour or a relaxing weekend to a genuine Danish meal in Denmark.

I must tell you about my visit to Denmark. Was it a ghost town? With the exception of a modern grain elevator, most buildings in Denmark and

The Woody House Bed-and-Breakfast in Lincoln

Lower Denmark were vacant, yet they were neat and appeared to be in good repair. I knocked on doors of nearby residences just outside of town without success and was about to give up when a battered farm truck came roaring down a drive. Seeing my perplexity the driver stopped. It was Ruth Sorensen on the way to a doctor with several children. Ruth typifies the friendly spirit here. Even though she didn't have time to show me the sights of Denmark she insisted on introducing me to a neighbor, Susan Mollerskov, who would assist me.

Well, Susan was waiting for the Fed Ex man, so she couldn't leave her house, but she did tell me a lot about the town: the Wade *huset* (house) listed on the State Register of Historic Places, Denmark Lutheran Church on the National Register of Historic Places, the Danke Hus (a Danish specialty gift shop), Elsie's Old Fashioned Herb and Flower Garden, plus the nearby Spillman Creek Lodge Bed-and-Breakfast.

Once more the magnetic charm of the county came up in conversation. Susan said, "It's the rolling hills and the quiet countryside that transform a tour into an experience that is almost spiritual."

Susan and her husband live in an old hotel in Denmark. They came from Kansas City to be married in the little Denmark Lutheran Church, and they honeymooned in the hotel they now live in. In Kansas City they felt irresistibly drawn back to the tranquil ambience of Denmark, and so it became their home.

If in Lincoln during the summer, put Vernon and Elfrieda Schneider's farm on your itinerary. Their farm has been featured in many magazines as one of the prettiest in the country. Hidden in a valley are rampant flowers and rustic barns.

For a laid-back day or two or perhaps a week, call one of the local bed-and-breakfasts and let them help you plan a time that may well change your life. Take some time to hear the message of the hills. Take a leisurely drive down country roads, windows open to hear the meadowlark's song and its little cousin the dickcissel. Listen for the pert, pert scolding call of a nighthawk.

Walk in the prairie at dawn, sit under a cottonwood, and watch the Smoky Hill haze dissolve as the sun reaches its zenith. Marvel at the mystery.

Lindsborg
Valkommen Till Little Sweden

Picture a little village nestled in a green valley; a thin smoky haze brushes the surrounding hills, and the warm morning sun at your back glows on the brilliant white of a church steeple and granaries. A deep blue sky rules overhead. A sign near this vantage point on Smoky Valley Road reads, "Valkommen Till Little Sweden."

Old-country charm and Kansas hospitality greet everyone who comes to Lindsborg, a unique Kansas town. It may be known as Little Sweden, but it's much more than a Swedish cultural replication. While Swedish influences are strong, maybe even dominant, Lindsborg has its own identity, its own creative essence. This little town of 3,001 people is literally alive with the sound of music, vibrant colors, and vivacious people.

Speaking about the artistic and creative ambience of Lindsborg, Dorene Anderson, executive director of the Chamber of Commerce, remarked, "Swedish people love song and beauty.... They [the pioneers] came to Kansas to do more than just eke out a living."

Lindsborg is world renowned for Bethany College's Eastertime presentation of George Frideric Handel's *Messiah*, performed annually since 1882. Its reputation for excellence has brought national media attention to the Messiah Festival. Lacking musical instruments, the original seventy-five performers used tuning forks at rehearsals. A thirteen-member orchestra was imported from Rock Island, Illinois, for the final performances. Today the Bethany College Oratorio Society numbers 350 singers and 55 instrumentalists.

Ten art galleries, including the prestigious Birger Sandzen Memorial Art Gallery, and twenty-four delightful shops bear out Dorene's statement—Lindsborg's people love art and they love to share it with visitors. A great Dala Horse welcomes you to Hemslojd, a Swedish shopping adventure. Partners Ken Sjogren and Ken Swisher always have a gallery of watchers as they carve and paint Dala Horses. While working they tell about the Swedish Dala Horse and Swedish Holiday Apple Tree traditions.

Across the street at Prairie Woods you can see displayed the craftsmanship of Swedish-American artist Gene Applequist. His handmade Swedish motif furniture is recognized as among the finest on this side of the Atlantic—it's simply beautiful. Also in the Prairie Woods gallery you may find artist Rita Sharpe painting folk art dinner plates featuring a "kurbit" motif (a Swedish eighteenth-century floral style), or sculptor John Whitfield and other artists at work. Personal contact with an artist makes personalized art possible—your name or anniversary date,

Picnic spot on Coronado Heights overlooking Lindsborg

for example, on your purchase.

The philosophical comments of artist Norman Malm at the Anton Pearson Woodcarving Studio are an inspiration for anyone who loves folklore. He creates lovely little tomtes, legendary elflike creatures that are said to protect rural folks. Usually Norman's tomtes wear red nightcaps over flowing white hair, but their garments can be personalized to suit particular occupations or pastimes.

Artist Maleta Forsberg paints and draws her inspirations, many of them natural landscapes and wildlife. Her work appears in the Courtyard Gallery and at her lovely Olive Springs Schoolhouse Gallery in the nearby Smoky Hills. One evening a number of years ago, just before Christmas, V.Lee and I drove out to the Schoolhouse Gallery. In the darkness colored Christmas lights and candles in the windows softly illuminated the old one-room schoolhouse through gently falling snow.

Recently I asked Maleta about the unusual creative spirit found in Lindsborg. She replied, "The love of art may trace back to the long, lonely arctic nights in the old country; bright colors and wood to carve warmed the heart. And then again, maybe it was the influnce of Birger Sandzen."

The influences of Swedish bright colors and of Birger Sandzen are readily apparent in Lindsborg today. The radiant Swedish blues, greens, reds, and golds make Lindsborg storefronts and banners different from the decor in other towns. Whether it was the almost mystic creative Lindsborg ambience that kept eminent artist Birger Sandzen in Kansas, or whether his influence created the Lindsborg mystique, is not clear. Nevertheless, though trained in Stockholm and Paris and featured in prestigious American and European art exhibitions, Sandzen devoted sixty years of his life to Bethany College and Lindsborg. The Birger Sandzen Memorial Gallery in Lindsborg displays Sandzen's bold "colorism" as well as the work of many other artists.

V.Lee and I had a delightful time Christmas shopping in Lindsborg; the only problem for me was getting V.Lee out of some of the shops. At Main Street Toys, I think, she was vicariously reliving her youth as she shopped for granddaughters Alyssa and Sofia; at the Gnome Home it was an infatuation with the little gnomes; and at the Kitchen Shop both of us enjoyed conversation with owners Viki and Ray Kahmeyer (his pottery is on display there). A parade down Main Street, led by blinking and whistling fire trucks, included children in costume, children riding wagons pulled by ponies, plus llamas, horses, dogs, and Santa Claus. It kept me busy capturing the color and excitement on film.

Among the frequent special events in Lindsborg are Svenk Hyllningsfest (honoring Swedish pioneers), Millfest (the 1898 Smoky Valley Roller Mill springs back to life), Lucia Festival (reliving a legend), 1996 Swedish Immigration Jubilee, Messiah Festival, Midsummer's Day Festival, Broadway RFD, plus a host of exhibitions and folk dancers and much music.

Furniture made of pine imported from Sweden and hand-stitched quilts lend authenticity to your stay in the Swedish Country Inn downtown. Enjoy a breakfast "taste" of Sweden—Swedish tea rings, rusks, knackbrod, pickled herring, beets, meatballs, assorted cheeses, fresh fruit, hard-boiled eggs, lingonberries, and lots of coffee. For Swedish lunch and dinner cuisine—Svenska Kottbullar, Pytt i panna, Helgeflundra, and more—try the Swedish Crown Restaurant and the Brunswick Hotel Restaurant.

History buffs love the Old Mill Museum Complex right on the Smoky Hill River. The Smoky Valley Roller Mill (erected in 1898 and restored to full operating condition in 1981) and the Swedish Pavilion (prefabricated in Sweden for display at the 1904 St. Louis World's Fair and later moved to Lindsborg) are stellar attractions here. Other features include a museum, an 1870 log cabin, and a Santa Fe steam locomotive.

Valkommen Till Little Sweden.

Linn County
Marsh of the Swans

Following the dawn light west through the Marsh of the Swans, skirting Boicourt. . . by a walnut savannah, around hills, and on random roads I discovered the heart of Linn County. There is a local legend of two lovers, an Indian princess and a great chief lost in raging waters as they fled from her irate father. In time they emerged from the waters as two snow-white swans, returning every spring. According to the legend, Longfellow's Evangeline on her troubled quest saw the swans and said "Marais des Cygnes" (Marsh of the Swans)—thus the name of the river and the area that is now a wildlife refuge.

Population is sparse in Linn County, only a little over eight thousand. Mound City, the county seat, is home to about eight hundred. The county is charming, innocently pastoral. I sense that people here believe they are missing out on modern life, not realizing that they are living the authentic experience that many in our society crave today. It almost seems that peace and harmony are inherent in Linn County, except for the legacy of the Trail of Death and the saga of Bleeding Kansas.

In the fall of 1838 the federal government removed a band of Potawatomi Indians from their home near the Great Lakes in Indiana. Their forced march ended after sixty-one days of hardship and thirty-nine deaths. The Trail of Death, now an official Regional Historical Trail, ended at St. Mary's Mission in present-day Linn County.

Today a shrine celebrating the life of Saint Philippine Duchesne stands on the site of the old mission. Rose Philippine Duchesne, a French nun, arrived at St. Mary's in 1841 to minister to Trail of Death survivors. Archaeological explorations have uncovered home-site foundations and many artifacts. Kansas explorers of any faith will discover a spiritual vibrancy here as they walk the wooded paths along Sugar Creek and contemplate the history of this spot. You'll find traces of the old road to California here as well.

Tangible evidence of Bleeding Kansas–era violence and atrocities blend into the prairies and woods of Linn County as if they were part of the natural scene. At the Marais des Cygnes

Stone house at the Marais Des Cygnes Massacre Park

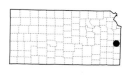

Massacre Memorial Park a nondescript ravine marks the spot where proslavery leader Charles Hamelton and twenty-nine followers lined up eleven free-state neighbors and shot them in cold blood. A month later John Brown arrived there and built a fort on the site.

In October of 1864 the largest Civil War cavalry battle west of the Mississippi River erupted several miles south of the present-day town of Pleasanton. A Confederate army of seven thousand men was routed by twenty-five hundred Union cavalry. The Confederates were encumbered by wagonloads of plunder, a herd of cattle, and a flock of sheep that Confederate General Sterling Price deemed important. A heavy rain the night before made the banks of Mine Creek difficult to negotiate with the heavy wagons of booty. Today a visitor center is being built on the battlefield site.

The Linn County Historical Museum in Pleasanton displays Battle of Mine Creek memorabilia. A life-size diorama depicts the capture of Confederate General John Marmaduke by Union Private James Dunlavy, whose great-grandson posed for the reproduction. The museum features an old-fashioned general store that reminds me of our hometown grocery store in the early thirties—the spool of white twine, the roll of wrap-

Civil War reenactor at the Mine Creek battle site

ping paper, the coffee grinder with its big flywheels, and a big supply of candy corn.

The most somber reminders of the struggle 130 years ago lie in the little cemetery at Trading Post and National Cemetery Number One in Mound City. The little village of Trading Post on U.S. 69 claims to be the oldest Kansas settlement still in existence. The Trading Post Museum has a copy of a map produced by a Belgian cartographer in 1825 showing the "Establishment de Chouteau" on the Marais des Cygnes River. The nearby Trading Post School, circa 1886, is still used for elections and the annual county spelling bee. I spent most of my time there in the antique farm machinery building. When I see an old threshing machine I just love to tell my "how hard we worked on the threshing crew" stories to any willing bystander.

A military road, roughly paralleling modern U.S. 69, was built about 1838 connecting Fort Leavenworth, Kansas, and Fort Gibson, Oklahoma. The road was intended to be the permanent divide between areas open to settlement and Indian territory. Many American Indian tribes, including the Potawatomi, were removed from the eastern states and promised permanent possession of the land west of the military road. In 1854, however, Kansas Territory was opened to settlement. Part of this military road still exists east of Pleasanton, and the narrow concrete strip of old Highway 69 just east of Trading Post covers the original military road.

As I walked by the Register of Deeds office in the Linn County Courthouse, built in 1886, I thought about all the transactions recorded in those musty books, representing 110 years of aspirations, heartaches, and drama. The jury room seemed most ominous. This courthouse in Mound City represents the passage of time to me; all who witnessed its earliest days, even the youngest children, are gone.

Linn County is fertile Kansas explorer territory. There are always subtle beauty and unexpected mystery over the hill or around the corner. Even in July, amid meadows and roadsides sprinkled with red clover, mullein, scurf pea, and brown-eyed Susan, the area was so lush green that a red cardinal in flight seemed garish.

Lyons/Rice County
Coronado Didn't Get the Picture

Does the West begin on the outskirts of Lyons in Rice County, or maybe just across Cow Creek? I almost think so. The cozy cluster of shops around Lyons's courthouse square suggests eastern space-consciousness; going west out of town the horizon expands, broken only by isolated grain elevators and Roosevelt's Chinese elms.

A Quiviran Indian display in the Coronado-Quivira Museum

I enjoyed exploring Lyons and Rice County. I have been there many times, but this time I was looking for special insight, for nuances I thought you might enjoy. Downtown Lyons is full of such special places within a block or two of the city square.

The whole family will feel like explorers at the Coronado-Quivira Museum. For instance, did you know that five hundred years ago more people lived in Rice County than today? When Coronado arrived here in 1541 he found an agrarian people living in permanent homes. You'll see a full-size replica of a Quivira Indian lodge here along with Coronado and Santa Fe Trail artifacts plus an outstanding Stan Herd Mural. The museum is a "must see" for every Kansan.

To find the museum, look for a mother reading a storybook to her children on a park bench. Don't worry, she'll be there. This heartwarming life-size bronze sculpture is by George Lundeen.

The shops around the square are fun to visit. I found myself drawn into friendly conversations and even a purchase because the sales clerk took the time to explain the product (a special small-town advantage). The doughnut shop is delightful (but caloric—an exploration hazard Coronado didn't face). The pharmacy offers gifts of every kind (including post cards for my granddaughters), plus a wealth of information. Another shop is full of little treasures and creatures: Hummels, Gnomes, Precious Moments, and more. A nearby deli—soups, salads, pizza—is just right for a lunch break.

The sign at Hollinger's Antiques said, "Warning, antique pox is contagious." I was smitten; I liked the building, an old lumberyard with lots of space, hidden lofts, and corners. I begged for a ride on the old freight elevator, but that was a no-no; liability laws, you know.

Westward ho to Raymond, population 125. Judy Hayes says she might well be the only female owner of a windmill service in the world. She and her foreman, Larry Backstrom, told me one windmill story after another; in fact, they started a boom truck and picked up a windmill just for a photo. Somehow in a pasture a windmill fits into the natural world. It responds to the prairie wind, pulsates like a heart, and draws water from the soil like a tree.

I ran into a parking problem in Alden, population 185. Cars, with tags from all across the state, were parked near a place called Prairie Flower Crafts. Inside, like bees after pollen, shoppers were looking at and feeling designer fabrics, silk flowers, baskets; pushing shopping carts loaded with colorful bolts of cloth; and lining up at the cash register. Can you imagine three adjoining early 1900s stores—recessed fronts, tin ceilings, wood floors, screen doors—

all very functional, housing a quilter's, designer's, and homemaker's paradise? Sara Fair Sleeper, the owner, welcomes you.

For the Spanish Conquistadors crossing the prairies 450 years ago, the windmills of Raymond and the golden fabrics of Alden might have seemed like the realization of the Impossible Dream, and drovers on the nearby Santa Fe Trail might well have said, "Why go on to Santa Fe?"

When you follow remnants of the Santa Fe Trail, see if you can envision Rice County as a treeless plain? Can your new explorer eyes see the mixed-grass prairie—tall and short grasses—and flowers as colorful as Sara's fabrics? I was lucky enough to have Wilmer Ekholm, a farmer on the trail, guide me to the Marker Cottonwood. He verbal-

ly painted a vivid picture for me of the old trail and vanished stone corral. The Marker Cottonwood (about two hundred years old) is still standing where the trail crossed the Little Arkansas River. Nearby at the Cottonwood Cemetery, depressions in a pasture mark grave sites of soldiers who once guarded the trail, as well as rifle pits where they crouched during raids.

Plows have pretty well eliminated evidence of the Santa Fe Trail, but west of Chase ruts left by the trail are still visible in several pastures. The ruts appear as swales about twelve to thirty feet wide. For best photo results use either early-morning or late-afternoon sunlight to provide shadow detail. Ralph Hathaway has seven parallel swales in his pasture. He is an excellent trail

resource person.

At the Cow Creek crossing a well was dug either by soldiers stationed there or by Buffalo Bill Mathewson in the 1860s. The well, known as Buffalo Bill's well, is still there, capped by a steel plate. It's a pretty spot easily accessible; a place to read about a skirmish and to contemplate the changes wrought by five hundred years. Quiviran Indians, Coronado, William Becknell, the Buffalo Bills (Mathewson and Cody), George Custer, and countless drovers, troops, pioneers, and farmers have left their footprints here on the sandy Cow Creek banks.

On Highway U.S. 56 west of Lyons a large cross has been erected to commemorate Father Padilla, martyred by Indians in 1542. Apparently the Native Americans didn't like the idea of his coming six thousand miles to tell them what to do.

Oh, I must not forget to mention the Lyons Christmas star and bell. What a pleasant sight on a cold December night to see a star and bright red bell hovering on the horizon as one approaches Lyons. For years the bell and star graced the courthouse spire, but in 1951 they were enlarged and placed on the water tower. Sixteen hundred feet of wire form the bell, which is 160 feet in circumference. A time-exposure photo here will make a nice Christmas card.

The "Marker" cottonwood on the Santa Fe Trail

McPherson
They Built Bigger and Better

Can you keep a secret? Well, I'll tell you one. McPherson is so special, so perfect, that we don't want the world to know about it, lest they take it away from us. In McPherson, spring flowers are prelude to a lovely May fete; on summer evenings families stroll serenely along tree-lined avenues; Christmastime means candles in the courthouse windows; and always people greet each other in friendly fashion.

Commerce is McPherson's key rural culture element—ten of its businesses are on the Fortune 500 list. Always well kept, the city seems immune to severe fluctuations in the national economy. In fact, nearby booming oil fields helped McPherson weather the Great Depression in style. A diversity of manufacturing plants, a major insurance company, a refinery, and agriculture stabilize the economy. Today McPherson is a leading center for the manufacture of plastic products and associated production equipment.

White prairie grain castles and the stately old courthouse dominate the skyline; attractive industrial plants and prosperous farms surround the city; and McPherson's Main Street, parks, schools, and homes reflect the American dream.

It all started in the early 1870s when four men of Scottish descent from Salina and eight others organized a town company. They named the company for a Civil War hero, General James Birdseye McPherson. A McPherson Scottish Society and a colorful pipe band (whose members parade in kilts) maintain the Scottish connection to this day.

Considering McPherson's roots, it's no wonder that the city is vital and robust. The city became a melting pot of many cultures, while Swedish Lutherans and Dutch and Swiss Mennonite immigrants plowed McPherson County prairies. McPherson's leaders had extraordinary vision, always challenging the status quo. They built bigger and better, drilled oil wells, synthesized diamonds, established refineries—but always, quality of life came first.

An ambitious group attempted to move the state capital to McPherson in 1887. Six passenger coaches loaded with state legislators arrived at the McPherson train station on February 19 of that year. The visitors were royally entertained in the Persian Room of the Union Hotel and in the "old" opera house. A Main Street building (on the west side of the 300 block) still wears the inscription "Capital Block 1887" above its cornice. Today, few people in McPherson realize that the "old" opera house and some evidence of its second-floor theater remain on a Main Street corner.

A new, bigger, and better opera house incorporating the latest technology—electric lights—was built in 1888. This impressive three-story brick structure topped with triangular pediments and turrets has much to tell about early McPherson. The varied stone window trim outside and the ornate capitals on columns inside proclaim, "Look at us, we're the finest." Tattered old playbills plastered on a wall indicate not just highbrow opera but melodramas, medicine shows, and acrobats as well. In the cellar, pre-courthouse jail cells are almost hidden. Then there are the underground passageways that supposedly wended their way beneath the city. Oh, what stories they could tell!

I got goose bumps peering into the darkened tunnel remnant. It's said that the stars of the shows made their way underground from the Union Hotel to their dressing rooms in the opera house. Whatever the

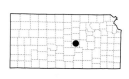

McPherson bagpipers add a Scottish accent to many events

reality, it would be exciting to retrace some of the old passageways. The McPherson Opera House is now in the process of restoration following many years of neglect.

The McPherson County Courthouse, built in 1894, is another demonstration of the pioneer spirit and vision that continue to this day. Recently, as I meandered through the courthouse admiring the excellent renovation work done in 1981, I noticed a door ajar on the third floor. Curious, I opened it. It was a stairway up to the clock tower. Uneasily I entered and clambered up the steps to a point just below the clock works where a trap door barred my way. I could feel the age of the structure here; no veneer of plaster and wood separated me from the elemental stones placed here by workmen long dead.

My little escapade led me to appreciate the work of John Casebeer more fully. In 1972 the clock stopped and the county commis-

sioners let bids for the repair. The costly bids were rejected; in typical McPherson spirit sixty-five-year-old Commissioner Casebeer said, "Let me take a look at the clock." Casebeer climbed the hundred-foot tower several times, saw the problem, made new parts, started the clock, and charged the county $7.50.

I wouldn't believe it if I couldn't see it. Exhibited in the McPherson Museum is the jawbone of a shovel-tusk mastodon found near Canton, Kansas, in 1936. It looks like the tusk of an elephant with a flat shovel added on. Nearby is a nine-foot imperial mammoth tusk. Upstairs is the world's first synthetic diamond, made by Dr. Hershey at McPherson College in 1926. The most interesting exhibit I saw here was a cross-section of an oak tree that grew here from 1778 to 1934. Keyed to the growth rings is a chronology starting with the Revolutionary War and ending with McPherson's founding.

Of course, McPherson does

not live in the past; its roots engendered values and aspirations that created today's high standards and quality of life. The latest edition of *The 100 Best Small Towns in America* by Norm Crampton ranks McPherson thirty-third. Robert MacPherson, past executive vice president of McPherson's Chamber of Commerce, has this to say: "I was raised in Pennsylvania and spent most of my life in the military. . . traveled all over the world. When we approached retirement we consulted Crampton's book and discovered a field of diamonds here in McPherson. We love it; it is home."

Visiting and shopping McPherson Main Street are a delightful adventure. For example, Belli Brothers Music Services displays model trains in the basement—over twelve hundred feet of free-lance *HO* track and an *N*-scale Santa Fe run from Hutchinson to Dodge City. The Cook's Nook is really a gourmet cook's emporium, and the historic ambience and great cuisine of the Main Street Deli make it the perfect place for you to experience McPherson's warm congeniality.

McPherson is simply a wonderful place to visit, to live, and to do business. Thirty-three restaurants, motels with super convention facilities, a bed-and-breakfast, and a mobile home court welcome you always.

Marion
Greeting the Dawn Walking Hand in Hand

How about a dawn Flint Hills excursion to start your exploration of Marion and its environs? One morning in early June, V.Lee and I parked on a hillcrest somewhere east of Marion, far from highway noise, waiting for the sunrise. With the car windows open, the morning air carried in the lowing of a cow, a calf responding, the wonderful clunk of a windmill, and, as the light broke on the horizon, an increasing chorus of birds. Hand in hand, camera slung over my shoulder, we walked toward the dawn. The kingbirds were waking up; I love the the way they chatter at dawn. We heard the clarion call of a sandpiper on its fence post perch and watched its trilling throat bobble.

Every time I see it, I marvel at the magic of morning light sweeping over a valley, revealing grasses and a multitude of wildflowers, and at retreating shadows outlining gentle hillside contours.

Dawn comes early, but what if you woke up in the middle of all this, say at Country Dreams Bed-and-Breakfast northeast of Marion? This lovely new farm home has five guest rooms, private baths for each, and large rooms for meetings, and when you step outside the natural world is there for you.

Personally I don't think anything can top the Flint Hills experience, but there's more here in Marion County than flora and fauna. There are the wonderful people, the creative things they do, and the influence of the land on the people.

The copper art created by farmer/rancher Ern Hett is the beauty of the hills translated into metal. The blue flame of Hett's welding torch turns copper stock into sunflowers, sheaves of wheat, and butterflies. He can take discarded implement parts and convert them into herons and grasshoppers. If your timing is right you may see him at work. The Copper Shed, Hett's workshop and display room on his ranch, blends into the surrounding grasslands and wildflowers that abound there. Our daughter Liz, a professional graphic artist, makes an annual sojourn from her Salt Lake City home to visit this wonderful display.

The influence of the Flint Hills and their foundation of ancient stone is very apparent in the city of Marion. In fact,

Upland sandpipers arrive every spring in the Flint Hills

the town is often referred to as "Stone City" because its older buildings are built of rock quarried in the Flint Hills. Dates on Main Street stone facades read 1886, 1887, and 1893.

The Hill School Building, circa 1873, is the oldest school house still in use in Kansas today. Now it houses high school classrooms and administrative offices. This large multi-story limestone structure was originally the home of Kansas School District Number One. District boundaries extended south to Oklahoma and west to Colorado in the late 1860s.

Another massive Marion limestone structure is the Elgin Apartments, constructed in 1886 and operated as the Elgin Hotel till the 1950s. The county courthouse, built in 1907 of native limestone and Bedford Indiana stone, is listed on the National Historic Register along with the Hill School and the Elgin Apartments.

Whether or not some intrinsic Flint Hills vitality conceives artistic energy I do not know, but an appreciation of the arts is obvious in Marion. Summer events in beautiful Central Park and products in downtown shops reflect a response to the beauty of the hills.

Every second Saturday evening, May through August, there's a free Summerfest variety performance (that might include a Will Rogers impersonator, clowns, jazz, country music, and more) on the Luta Creek stage in the park. Tall bur oaks and cottonwoods form a natural canopy over Central Park's children's playground and fountains. Old-fashioned globe lights accentuate the green lawns. A lighted nature trail follows Luta Creek.

A lump of clay spinning into an artistic bowl on a potter's wheel always intrigues me. You can see pottery work in progress at the Flint Hills Clay Works in Marion. As I watched Paula Miller "throw" a squishy globule, she explained, "Guys have an advantage in this work. It actually takes a lot of muscle to form the clay as the wheel spins." Her deft fingers, however, made it look easy. Flint Hills Clay Works not only produces fine pottery but also blends and markets over a million pounds of clay annually for other potters and schools. Group tours are welcome.

I discovered that there's gold to be found in the Flint Hills, but I did my prospecting at Flint Hills Gold in Marion. The gold here is not just a selection of jewelry but also the opportunity to have Beverly Schor design jewelry that is uniquely yours, perhaps incorporating a creative idea of your own. She also reproduces antique jewelry.

I couldn't resist a Santa Fe Trail side excursion from Marion. It was a hot, windy summer day as I drove out to Lost Springs, a Santa Fe Trail site west of the town of Lost Springs. It was a situation in which I needed my new Kansas explorer eyes. The story was there on faded sign boards—a watering place from 1804 to 1872, ruts across the road, a hotel and tavern, at times two hundred wagons encamped in circles here, and in 1878 seventeen cowboys lost in a blizzard—but it was up to me to transform this hot, now barren place into a point of interest.

Tramping to a small grove of trees, I found a spring-fed brook. A century and a half ago this little oasis was the equivalent of a gas station, restaurant, and motel to travelers. I wasn't sure I had found the trail ruts mentioned on the nearby sign, but the wind blowing in the grasses spoke of a traveler's encounter with awesome solitude long ago.

Back in Marion, "the city between two lakes," the traveler glories in comparative paradise. On the shore drive around Marion County Lake I discovered the Kingfisher Inn overlooking the lake. The menu included traditional American cuisine and a delicious light menu.

You'll find great pleasure in exploring Marion. Don't forget the camping and water recreation offered at Marion Reservoir.

Maxwell Wildlife Refuge
The Arch of the Azure Heavens

On a Sunday evening last July V.Lee and I enjoyed the grandest show we have ever seen. The stage was two thousand acres of green, rolling prairie land accented with an array of goldenrod and daisy fleabane. The background was the endless circle of a far horizon stretching 93 million miles to the setting sun. The proscenium arch of the azure heavens towered over us with subtle hues of purple and orange descending to the horizon.

I could go on this way, describing an orchestra of meadowlarks and nighthawks and a speechless cast of more than two hundred, but V.Lee says I overdramatize. I did hear one member of the audience say the evening was a spiritual experience. I'll get on with the story.

Maxwell Wildlife Refuge begins six miles north of Canton in McPherson County. It covers four sections of the Smoky Hills and, with the exception of the McPherson State Fishing Lake, is fenced in as a buffalo and Rocky Mountain elk refuge. (The word *buffalo* is actually a misnomer. The correct word is *bison.*) This pristine tract is large enough for the animals to roam freely and to be viewed in a natural setting. Usually about two hundred buffalo and sixty elk are on the refuge.

A public road crosses through the refuge via cattle guard gates (no gates to open,

you just drive across). Often the buffalo herd may be viewed here in close proximity. There is also a viewing tower to see animals and landscape. The most intimate way, however, to experience the refuge is to ride the weekend tram tour. (There is a small charge, and reservations are a good idea.)

Della and Owen Meier, true lovers of the prairie, conduct the tours. Why do they devote their time to the refuge?

Della Meier hosts a tram ride at the Maxwell Game Refuge

"We like it; it's more important than eating.... It's kind of a religion with us—showing God's world," Owen said. "Wildlife could live without us, but we can't live without it."

Before the tram departs, Owen chases around in his Jeep locating the herd. One of three alternative routes usually brings the tram in close to the buffalo. The elk are more reclusive, harder to get close to except in the winter season when supplemental range cubes are fed to elk and buffalo. The male elk's racks (antlers) reach full size in October and are shed in May. The eerie bugling call of an elk bull can be heard here in September and October.

Excitement reminiscent of the Old West comes back to Maxwell every November—rangers round up the buffalo, fences and crude corrals strain as the herd is sorted in preparation for the annual buffalo auction. Bewildered yearlings, cows, and bulls circle the pens, wary rangers climb fences, as the auctioneer's chant goes on. In 1994 you could have bought a buffalo bull calf for $800 and a heifer for $1,300. Bring your trailer or just come to enjoy this unique event. Buffalo burgers are sold at lunchtime.

The auction is the real world, the herd roaming the Smoky Hills almost seems an apparition, yet in reality the land can

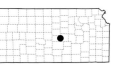

Visitors enjoy up-close buffalo encounters in Maxwell

support only so many animals. The hard fact is that sound range management demands culling. The auction replaces the mountain lion and the bear who, you might say, managed the prairie long ago.

Last fall a friend and I came out to Maxwell just before sunrise. The sounds of dawn preceded the light, and we heard what we had come to hear: a short bellow, a whistle—almost like a scream—and some grunts. The bugle call of a bull elk muffled by the morning mist is a primeval sound, something that revives ancient memories. As the sky brightened we saw big ears reaching up over a hill. A

female elk came in and out of view as she skirted some hills. Suddenly we were aware of shadowy forms stalking her. Through binoculars we saw four or five coyotes. What they were up to we never discovered.

V.Lee and I usually come up to Maxwell in the spring to see the wildflowers. Della says that at least sixty varieties are found here. Kansas may not be as dramatic as the seashore, but in detail it can be more beautiful. Walk up to a blue indigo early while the dew still clings. Look very closely. Can't you almost see the beauty of the whole world, especially when the sun catches a dewdrop? The color of

the petal: is it blue, is it purple? Or must you call it "lapis lazuli"?

You can never see all there is to see in Maxwell; it changes with the seasons and the weather. Since these buffalo cannot migrate to greener pasture for the winter, they are fed supplemental range cubes. A morning ride through the snow to feed these animals is an experience. The truck bounces over the hills till the herd is sighted. Once the buffalo see the truck they come running. It's awesome to see for the first time animals weighing two thousand pounds charging toward your frail little truck. The animals surround the truck; you can smell them and hear their guttural conversation. By the buffalo's size you might expect to hear a deep, roaring voice, but I've never heard more than a snorting, inhaling grunt, something like that of a pig.

On that wonderful late afternoon in July, the regal majesty of a bull buffalo, arrayed in his fine fur, standing almost golden in the sunlight, required no fanfare or eloquent words. Bulls and cows and calves, dotting the green hillside, spoke to the heart.

There is so much to explore in Maxwell. You'll find basic camping facilities, fishing, and hiking at the adjoining state lake. Nearby Canton and McPherson provide all the services, food, and lodging you'll require.

Meade

The Daltons Ride Again

It didn't take me long to discover which visitor attraction is promoted the most in Meade, Kansas. The Dalton Gang hideout and its infamous escape tunnel bring in tourists by car, van, and bus every day except major holidays.

The 1887 romance and marriage of Eva Dalton and John Whipple initiated tales of suspicion and intrigue that still linger in the peaceful town of Meade. The Whipples moved into a little cottage in the southeast corner of Meade right after the wedding. "They say" that shortly after the marriage Mr. Whipple abandoned his commercial pursuits to play poker seriously and Eva closed her millinery shop to prance around town with a new carriage and fancy horses. The strange thing was that she always had different horses.

Meanwhile her brothers Bob and Grat Dalton gave up their jobs as deputies for the court of "Hanging Judge" Parker. At about the same time, someone began robbing trains and banks as well as stealing horses from California to Kansas. Rumors spread about the Daltons, but apparently no one ever discovered the secret Dalton Gang rendezvous in Meade.

After the Daltons' disastrous Coffeyville attempt to rob two banks at once and the killing of Grat and Bob, the Whipples quietly sneaked out of Meade. The story is that subsequent tenants of the house noticed strangers tying up horses near their barn and at times mysteriously appearing out of nowhere in their kitchen. Hidden trap doors and a tunnel from house to barn were finally discovered.

In the 1940s federal WPA workers helped the Meade Chamber of Commerce restore this legendary tunnel and hideout. Today children have replaced outlaws scampering through this well-lit ninety-five-foot tunnel. Of course, adults too enjoy a brief vicarious desperado experience walking underground from the horse barn (now a gift shop) and emerging from below into the Whipples' cozy cottage. The hideout provides a nice shaded playground and picnic area.

Exhibited also are an old steam tractor and several one-horse mail wagons. The mail wagons interested me because when I went to grade school many of my classmates arrived at school every morning in similar mail wagons.

The notoriety and drama of the Dalton hideout set me up to delve into another aspect of history at the Meade County Historical Society Museum. Among many excellent exhibits two especially attracted me. One was a sheep herder's wagon, probably never used in Kansas. Similar to a covered wagon, this vehicle provided in a very simple and compact way everything a man needed to live alone on a vast prairie with hundreds of sheep and a dog. That wagon makes an eloquent statement about a lonely life.

Also on display was a series of dust storm photos—not the best photography—but they told a compelling story. Someone younger than I might think the

A disc plow exhibited at the Meade County Museum

The Dalton Gang Hideout Museum in Meade

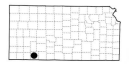

blackness of the roiling clouds exaggerated, but I can testify that a dust storm was awesome.

This is a modest museum in the sense that it does not over-dramatize hard times in Meade County. The truth is dramatic enough—two depressions, the dust bowl, and two world wars. The museum displays the various rooms typical of a 1910 Meade home as well as complete blacksmith, barber, harness, and other shops of that era.

I had a nice visit with Meade Mayor LeRoy Lemaster. We discussed the value of understanding the past to build the future. "We have one of the nicest museums; it's too bad that more people, especially children, don't come in," LeRoy told me.

Alfred Sawyer showed me another interesting facet of the museum, an outside exhibit. They have one of the larger displays of vintage farm implements in Kansas museums. I had fun with Alfred (another California convert to Kansas), asking him to explain functions of a disc plow and a stalk cutter. I wish some of

you old-timers would help their restorers match original colors to the machinery displayed. (This suggestion holds true for most museums. For an old farmer like me to see a McCormick mower painted green and yellow is disconcerting.)

I love this outside exhibit. A four-bottom plow here gives an old grandpa an opportunity to tell a little boy about long, hot days driving a model L Case tractor across the stubble fields. The Sunnydale one-room schoolhouse, a windmill, and a restoration shed are displayed here also. Thank you, Alfred, for a good show in spite of your

A mail wagon, Dalton Gang Hideout Museum

disc plow story.

Six flags have flown over Meade County since the time of Coronado: those of Spain, England, France, Mexico, Texas, and the United States. The six flags fly alongside U.S. 54 near the museum in downtown Meade.

Meade and Meade County are not glamour spots; they are the clean, solid, energetic fabric rural America is made of. Most of the area, slightly rolling pastures or cropland, is laid out with roads following a one-mile-square grid. Three cities are located in the county: Meade, population 1,527; Plains, population 957; and Fowler, population 571.

There is one exception to what I just said about glamour in Meade County. In Fowler's Neon 57 Cafe is a life-size image of Marilyn Monroe next to a '57 Chevy booth. For the fifties crowd this place will evoke many memories. Plains, on the other hand, is a down-to-earth farm town with grain elevators dominating the scene and the widest Main Street in the U.S.A. (155 feet, 5 inches).

Crime pays in Meade (the Daltons would never believe what they have done for the town) only in the historical sense. For a mini-vacation that will reaffirm your faith in rural culture, visit Meade. Good food, lodging, car services, and a nice park are there to welcome you.

Medicine Lodge
Exploring Romantic Legends of the Red Hills

"Yes, this is Kansas," I often say when I show my pictures of the Red Hills to audiences across the state. In Barber County west of Medicine Lodge the stereotypical image of Kansas as flat and barren falls and shatters like broken glass. Seen from a high vantage point at sunrise, the red mesas and buttes seem to float like an alien landscape above the predawn Kansas prairie below, defying time and space in any season. Brilliant red escarpments, often capped by contrasting whites or grays, contrast with deep green cedars and grasses of many seasonal hues. A closer look reveals layers of green shale and thin, translucent crystalline veins of satin spar, a variation of gypsum.

If you explore beyond nature's splendor, you will discover a vibrant human drama. By discovering special places such as Flower Pot Mound, the Twin Peaks, the Medicine River, and the Stockade you may vicariously relive the romantic legends and tales of adventure found in Barber County.

High adventure, indeed, is the history of Medicine Lodge. In early times this wondrous place was the land of the Kiowas; you can't blame them for wanting to keep it. Abundant water, grass, game of all kinds, and natural shelter made this beautiful land a paradise. The Native Americans considered the Medicine River holy because of its power to heal, and their belief has been confirmed by modern analysis of the waters. The story is that a medicine lodge, made of trees, rushes, and earth, served as a healing sauna when river water and herbs were placed on heated rocks.

In 1867 President Andrew Johnson issued a directive that the "Indian Menace" must be resolved. A "peace commission" was sent to parley with five Indian tribes: Kiowa, Arapaho, Cheyenne, Apache, and Comanche. The Indians insisted the meeting site be at the confluence of the Medicine River and Elm Creek. Thirty wagonloads of gifts were given to fifteen thousand Indians encamped nearby to induce them to cede their lands to the United States in exchange for reservation homes.

The Medicine Lodge Peace Treaty Pageant celebrates the signing of the 1867 peace treaty every three years in grand fashion. This huge outdoor show with a cast of more than twelve hundred compresses three hundred years of history into two hours of education and entertainment. The stage, a natural amphitheater of red cliffs, grassy plain, and wooded areas, covers more then forty acres. Thirty horse-drawn vehicles—oxcarts, bone wagons, and covered wagons—plus many, many horses support the cast. From a hilltop overlooking the stage, Kaye Kuhn, executive director of the pageant, described the spectacle to me. "A narrator tells the story as the action unfolds. You can see wagon trains approaching from that far hill, and you can see cowboys careening down that steep cliff over there." Proudly she added, "One of them is my boy." The next mega-show is in September 1997. Kaye is a great source of explorer information.

Adjoining the pageant grounds is the Kansas Championship Ranch Rodeo arena, acclaimed as one of the finest ranch rodeos anywhere. Last year twelve of the oldest and largest ranches in Kansas sent their top hands and horses to participate in this exciting rodeo. Events reflecting the work and the fun of authentic cowboys include

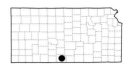

Dramatic red hues embellish the Red Hills

bronc riding, cattle doctoring, wild-cow milking, calf branding, ranch cutting, and double mugging.

I watched Kaye's husband, Earl Kuhn, watercolor artist at the Sagebrush Gallery, bring the Red Hills to life as he painted contemporary cowboys at work, authentically detailing their gear, the wildflowers, and the rich textures of the hills.

Kaye suggested a number of ways to intimately experience the ambience of the hills. The Gyp Hills (another name for the

Kasey Kuhn loves to provide Medicine Lodge information

Red Hills) auto tour starts three miles west of the city and meanders through this wonderful scenery for miles on country roads. Ask Kaye about another route that takes you through the almost-ghost towns of Lake City and Sun City. When in Sun City, even though the town looks abandoned, try the door at Buster's Bar and Grill. You'll love Buster; order a soft drink and ask him about Sun City.

If you have a horse or can borrow one Kaye has another super suggestion: a weekend Gypsum Hills trail ride sponsored by the Gant-Larson Ranch. Isolated from the modern world on this vast ranch you can experience on horseback the essence of the West as it was. Imagine the thrill of joining 250 riders to explore this unique and historic landscape.

"Nature's Poetry in Color" is a spring wildflower tour in the Red Hills sponsored by the Barber County Conservation Dis-

trict. V.Lee and I enjoyed one of these tours a few years ago, and our eyes were opened once again to the subtle beauty of the prairies. Somehow by learning the names of wildflowers I felt a greater appreciation for them.

A sundial? Why would I want to see a sundial? Because it's an equatorial sundial, a unique device that adjusts its time readout to follow the seasons. When I first saw it I thought it was broken because it appeared to be lying on its side. Not true; its large granite dial is parallel to the equator. Spring and summer shadows show on one side and fall and winter shadows on the other. You'll find it on the high school grounds.

Medicine Lodge was once enclosed by a stockade, and that's why you'll want to visit the Stockade Museum. Try to recreate in your mind what it must have been like to live within a stockade while you peruse the old cabin and many, many artifacts and photographs of the Medicine River valley. Another strange facet of Medicine Lodge history is told in the Carrie Nation home next to the stockade. Nation was the legendary hatchet-wielding temperance crusader of the late 1800s.

Medicine Lodge welcomes you with fine lodging, great food, and the Kiowa paradise.

Morland

A Mastodon Lumbers By on Shore

Charlotte Keith recognized a prehistoric rhinoceros tooth in a 4-H exhibit and wondered where the rest of the rhinoceros was. She found his jawbone protruding from an earthen embankment in an abandoned trench silo near Morland. Aware of the bone's fragile state she called for help from Fort Hays State University. Paleontologists began to dig and interest began to grow among neighbors, local and regional newspapers, and scientists. People from eighteen countries and finally the National Geographic Society began to dig also.

An image of a time long ago, some call it the Miocene Epoch, began to emerge: a stream running through subtropical flora almost familiar but yet quite different—grasses, bamboo, sedges, bulrushes, sunflowers, and even trees related to elm and hackberry. Strange-looking ducks and grebes swimming and flying are seen. Primitive toads, salamanders, and turtles bask on the shore. Suddenly a rhinoceros plunges into a pool, a mastodon lumbers by on the shore, and camels nibble on the trees.

This immemorial scene, hidden under the earth for millenia near Morland, Kansas, is expressed in bas-relief on the brick facade of the Citizens State Bank in Morland. Faye Minium, president of the bank and Charlotte's sister, commissioned artist Jack Curran to depict prehistoric life at the Minium Fossil Dig. Minium and Curran decided to use an ancient Babylonian art form known as sculpted wet brick. The result is an aesthetically pleasing work that any town in Kansas would be proud of.

An educational building over the dig site (similar to the one at the Dinosaur National Monument in Utah) is planned in coop-

Don Rowlison, curator of the Cottonwood Ranch

eration with the Sternberg Museum at Fort Hays State University.

On the lighter side, check out the display of 1950s comic books in the bank. The Lone Ranger, Red Ryder, and Roy Rogers ride again in 164 Golden Era Western and Adventure books matted and framed for your viewing pleasure.

After I finished photographing the bank's mural, Faye and husband Charlie invited me out to lunch, Morland style. Since the restaurant was closed we walked across the street to Bean's Country Store. Charlie picked up some turkey sandwiches and soft drinks and we joined some farmers having lunch around small tables. The wood floors creaked as farmers wearing John Deere and Co-op caps walked in. We discussed personal issues and the ambience that makes Morland so special. That the Miniums loved Morland and its 275 citizens was very obvious.

Later we toured the town. Faye and Charlie showed me the visitor center that was nearing completion in a restored building. From there we went down Main Street to a recently refurbished antique shop and into an old-fashioned dry-goods store. They told me about a new restaurant that would serve humongous hamburgers rivaling the famous Percy burgers once served in Morland. It's quite possible that the buns will

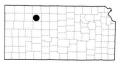

Metal art work created by David Brown of Morland

be in the shape of a rhinoceros.

Later Faye showed me a nature trail being developed for the Outdoor Wildlife Learning School. One of those old steel-truss bridges with a plank floor that rattles when you drive across has been moved in from another county to take the trail across a ravine.

Out in the suburbs north of town I stopped to visit my friend, metal artist David Brown. He pretends to be a commercial painter of tractors, trucks, and buses, but I know he's an artist at heart because of the way his eyes light up when he shows his latest creations, which are usually made out of discarded engine parts. Gears, shafts, sickles, seemingly random objects turn into abstract facsimiles of tractors, racers, birds, or flowers. Not all his art is abstract; under a

tarp was the outline of a 1947 Mack truck he was restoring. The joy his art brings to him is a pleasure to witness.

On down the highway, just past Studley, is a historical treasure, the Cottonwood Ranch. Original-ly known as the John Fenton Pratt Ranch, it is being restored by the Kansas State Historical Society. Established as a sheep ranch in the 1880s, the Cottonwood Ranch is an example of early ranch architecture with a touch of English influence united with local building materials.

We are very fortunate that people like Don Rowlison, the ranch curator, take the time to delve into the human drama that historic places like Cotton-wood Ranch represent. He tells the story of the ranch's founder, Abraham Pratt of Yorkshire County, England. Pratt, his two

sons, and two other Englishmen lived through the devastating winter of 1885-1886 in a one-room stone house so small that furniture had to be carried out at night to make room for the five men to sleep. The Pratts raised Merino sheep and pros-pered, though cattlemen suf-fered severe losses due to the blizzards of early 1886.

Abraham's son, John Fenton Pratt, enlarged the stone house and built the stone barns that make up the ranch today. John Fenton's wife broke into tears the first time she saw her new home, and during the first months of pioneer ranch life she repeatedly packed her bags and ran away while John was herding sheep.

Though life must have been difficult at the ranch, the beauty invested in the house speaks of love and higher aspirations. The massive Ogallala stone walls are trimmed at corners and around windows with Smoky Hills chalk limestone of varied hues ranging from bright yellow to a delicate rose. Pastel blue and white spindled porch posts and railings add to the charm.

Well, so it is in the Morland neighborhood. I still haven't told you about forlorn but enchanting Antelope Lake, or about the rumors of buried Spanish treasure (they say wild turkeys have been found with gold nuggets in their crops). I'll leave that exploration to you.

Nemaha County
Moments of Reflection—In Jail

Highway K-9 didn't seem to be in a hurry to go anywhere. It curved to the left and then to the right until I wasn't sure which way I was going. A big red combine loomed ahead, scattering mud and corn leaves on the road. I followed it about a mile before I could pass. Below me in a valley another combine was moving through a field harvesting eight rows at a brisk pace.

I made a swing through Wetmore and stopped by its famous jail. This little stone box must have been a terrible place to spend a night, but it's genuine. That's the way it was.

Later I turned into Corning on a white rock road, with dust preceding me into town. My eyes were drawn to a red brick building set high on a white stone foundation. A cupola topped a tower over the entry steps. Obviously quite old and very well kept, it struck my fancy.

The Farmers State Bank of Corning was built in 1892. Its president, Bob Niehues, told me, "Very few changes have been made throughout the years. We have the original blueprints right here on the wall to compare to." Tellers' cages, oak trim, cut glass, and stained windows, it's all there and still functioning as a bank today.

In Seneca, I went to jail. It was a moment for reflection— the ponderous levers that control the cell doors had an air of finality about them. The prisoners are long gone, but the Nemaha County Historical Museum recreates the past in the old Nemaha County jail and jailer's living quarters. It took a while to shift the focus to the other museum displays with those open cell doors staring at me.

Out of jail, I went looking for the second-largest hand-dug well in Kansas. It is large, thirty-four feet wide and sixty-five feet deep. So they say anyway. A fence and a dome guard the well, and it takes two keys to enter. Bill Miller, the Seneca Chamber of Commerce executive secretary, had only one key so I didn't get to see the well. Please call ahead when you come to Seneca so the keys to the well and to the city can be waiting for you.

Bill did help me find the 1922 Stutz fire truck and the Pony Express monument. Gleaming red with ornate white and twenty-four-carat gold-leaf trim, the Stutz is a restoration work of art, with its open cab, plush leather seat, running boards, wooden spoke wheels, lots of chrome levers (originally nickel), large searchlight, and polished ladders. Several blocks east a large glacial boulder and plaque commemorate the brief life of the Pony Express. Across the street a Pony Express Museum was being established.

I can't make up my mind about Fort Markley. It's a composite of authenticity, replica, and stereotype. Two early-day jails brought in from nearby towns are original and, together with other buildings, recreate the ambience of the Pony Express period. Enjoy a buffalo dinner in the Buffalo Cafe here and envision with your new explorer eyes the daring young Pony Express rider galloping into view.

Out in the country near St. Benedict, the lofty spire (172 feet

The Corning Bank, built in 1892 and still in business

tall) of St. Mary's church has raised eyes and aspirations for over a hundred years. Inside, the legendary beauty reflects the art of craftsmen who valued perfection more than time. I closed my eyes and tried to imagine the visual impact that St. Mary's on its hill and St. Bede, nestled in a valley near Kelly, must have made on the prairie before trees and other structures impaired the view.

Sabetha is a vibrant town and one in transition. Main Street hums with activity. The growing manufacturing sector vies with agriculture in the area's economy. Innovative manufactured products bring foreign markets and visitors to Sabetha. In transition, too, are the stores on Main Street. Neat gift shops carrying crystals, collectibles, gems, flowers, Kansas art, and more are thriving.

Maridel Wittmer, owner of the Village Sampler, says, "I closed a clothing store I operated for twenty-five years and opened the Sampler gift shop, and I'm very pleased with the change."

A county road led me to Albany (population zero, not to be confused with New Albany in Wilson County). This village is one of the best and most authentic collections of pioneer and turn-of-the-century buildings and artifacts in Kansas. Albany was a prosperous town until the railroad bypassed it and went through nearby Sabetha. Residents and businesses moved everything, including most buildings, to Sabetha.

A rock school house, Albany Rural District No. 1, is the only building here on its original site. Most of the other old buildings—a log cabin, a hundred-year-old farmhouse, a post office, a schoolhouse, and more—have been moved in from nearby small towns. A detailed replica of the Bern depot, several cabooses, and some track and rolling stock for rides add colorful variety. Modern machine sheds house antique farm machinery and tractors, old cars, and two airplanes built by the Red Bird Manufacturing Company of Bern, Kansas.

I've been to Albany's Old-Time Threshing Bee and Living History Show, where the screaming cry of a sawmill, the ring of hammer on anvil, the jingle of harness, and the booming of black-powder guns accompany spinning wheels, soap makers, and threshing machines in a giant step back in time. This time, though I missed the acrid smell of steam engines puffing, I was all alone. I tuned in to the haunting presence of men who drove square nails into old timbers, to lonely prairie women who manipulated hand-powered washers with children tugging at their skirts, and to the young teacher in a one-room school who faced gangling country boys nearly as old as she.

Make a day trip through Nemaha County. Observe the transition of farms and towns toward new technology. Barns and mom-and-pop grocery stores are becoming rare. Consider this: When, if ever, will the giant combines and trucks you meet become museum pieces?

A display of railroad equipment in Old Albany

Ness City
"The Settlers Were Cultured People"

When history describes an era at its inception, it is very near at hand in Ness County. Merely a lifetime ago, plus a generation or two, prairie winds swept unimpeded across the grassy plains.

"Today," says Ness City writer Jan Gantz, "you can drive out to a grassland hill near Ness City, stand there and still see it all as it was in the beginning: virgin sod never violated, the expanse of grass, the buffalo wallows. Look down—you may see a cavalry button or an arrowhead...."

The first settlers arrived in Ness County in 1873, but as you explore Ness City any image of pioneers living for years in crude dugouts will be shattered. Attesting to a taste for culture are structures built in the late 1880s: the recently restored Ness County Bank Building; the Beardslee Building, now housing a fine museum; the

The Lion Block, crumbling but defiant

Lion Block, crumbling but defiant; and the haunting remnants of an opera house. Local historian Ila Fritzler says, "The people that settled here were cultured people. Look at those old buildings, the design, the ornate trim. It was important to them to bring beauty to their new land."

Ness City is a bustling, vibrant town. Wheat trucks, cattlemen's four-wheelers, and oil-patch service trucks visually represent the area's commerce, and you can see a cross-section of the town's business community during morning coffee at the Balloon West or the Derrick Inn.

One evening last spring, as I relaxed in the Derrick Inn, it occurred to me how ideal Ness City is for someone craving a change of pace, a place to get away from daily stress. Just the drive to Ness City will slow the heart rate if you travel as a Kansas Explorer. Allow your new explorer eyes to see the

nuances of the seasons in the hills—the emerging wheat and bronze grasses of autumn, the purity of a winter snowscape, the verdant greens of spring contrasting with black earth prepared for seeding, and the wheatland gold of summer. Note the stone fenceposts dividing fields. Watch the people behind approaching windshields, see their friendly salutes. Let your eyes absorb the ever-changing hues of a Kansas sunset into your soul.

As the sun goes down, the tempo of life slows in Ness City. No bright lights beckon to the fast lane. Isolated by distance from the big cities, like an island port the motel is a haven for the night—dining in a cozy atmosphere, splashing in an indoor pool, luxuriating in a sauna, and slipping off to dreamland in a comfortable bed.

Greet the dawn east of the city; find a country-road hilltop, stop the engine, and listen. Each season brings different sounds—a coyote calling, a flight of geese or sandhill cranes, or a bawling calf. In early spring or autumn you may see frost creeping through the grass as the approaching dawn supercools the atmosphere. Marvel at the wonder of light (that had left the sun only eight minutes earlier) warming your face. Feel the earth under your feet and imagine the far horizon

Main Street, Arnold, Kansas

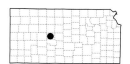

tilting toward the sun.

Back in Ness City enjoy breakfast in either of two welcoming cafes. Try to identify the farmer, the plumber, the banker, and the cabinet maker. Give the town a little time to wake up; but meanwhile, if you're a photographer, check out the old Ness County Bank Building at Main Street and Pennsylvania Avenue. Early-morning light brings out the rich hues of the native stone, and shadows accentuate the texture.

When completed in 1890 the bank building was called "the finest structure west of Topeka." Just imagine this four-story structure with its thirteen-foot ceilings, arched windows, and ornate stonework towering over

The 1890 Ness County Bank Building

virgin prairie land. Prairie Mercantile, a Kansas products store, is open weekday afternoons on the lower level. Here you can see and purchase fine hand-crafted merchandise consigned by Kansas artists and crafters.

Rumors about the old opera house led me to Cranmer's Woodworking Shop. I was greeted by the aroma of cedar, pine, and furniture stripper and a display of wood toys and a wood coffin in progress (order in advance). Brent Cranmer traced the history of the shop and the adjoining opera house back to the 1880s as he led me to an outside door next to the shop. An ancient ballroom-style stairway ascended to a ticket booth and a set of doors. You'll have to discover the rest of the story on your own.

And there's more to discover. In the office of the *Ness County News* is an old poster touting the Grand Interstate Canal that would run through Ness City. J. C. Hopper, a Ness City banker and promoter, envisioned this inland waterway that would have been large enough for steamboats and barges.

A drive in the country to nearby small towns is a bittersweet experience. The pastures and fields in spring are a luxuriant green, and in late June you'll see miles and miles of golden grain waiting to be stored in the white prairie castles towering over faded villages. The names Beeler, Utica, Arnold, and Brownell may pass into history, but the people who live there are resilient and they proudly call these towns home. A sign near Beeler points out George Washington Carver's homestead, but the invincible grassland has covered all traces of this brave and creative Ness County pioneer's past.

Touching on the plight of the rural community, Bill Sorenson, farmland management consultant, says, "Farms have grown larger—from an average of 480 acres in 1951 to a thousand acres now. From a population standpoint it's bad, but from necessity it's a given. Ness City may hold its own, maybe at the expense of the little communities in the county."

"Kansas is an undiscovered state," Ila Fritzler says. "The sunset, fireflies at night. . . . It's a great place to be, a diamond in the rough."

Discover why Fritzler and the people of Ness City fervently love their home town, with its grace, culture, and natural beauty.

Newton
The Legacy of Turkey Red

Take virgin prairie, rails of steel, the wickedest cattle town in the West, post-Civil War American entrepreneurs, pious Russian pioneers, and Turkey Red wheat. Mix these, let them simmer for 125 years while you stir in a depression, various wars, technological advances, and a sprinkle of diverse cultures.

This savory stew is Newton, Kansas—a wonderful place to explore. All the rural culture elements are there in full strength, including cuisine—to my great delight.

It all began when the Santa Fe Railroad crossed the Chisholm Trail in 1871 and someone said, "Let's call this place Newton." For a few years Newton was trail's end for the Texas cowboys. Hollywood and television glamorize this era, even though the reality was sweat, blood, dust, and mud. But people of vision saw the potential of fertile prairie earth and the Kansas climate. Those people made Newton what it is today. Settlers from the East and immigrants from foreign lands were enticed to come to central Kansas; among them were Mennonites, who brought the Turkey Red wheat.

History is alive and dynamic in Newton. The Old Mill Plaza, a reincarnation of the Monarch Steam Mill built in 1879, is home to a number of modern businesses and also features the Old Mill Restaurant and Bar.

The mill, saved from the wrecking ball by a last-minute midnight transaction, was restored in the mid-1970s by local inventor Lloyd Smith and his wife, Jaqueline. Meticulously rebuilt following original blueprints found in an old safe, the mill's unique mansard roof and brick smokestack once again dominate Newton's Main Street. Amid the elegant ambience, it's hard to believe that locomotives and train cars receiving flour once occupied the same room. A huge mural recreates this scene. Be sure to take the self-guided tour of the mill.

The old mill and the Warkentin House a few blocks away are part of the story of Bernhard Warkentin, who was instrumental in bringing the Mennonites and Turkey Red wheat to central Kansas. Warkentin, the son of a prominent Mennonite miller in the Russian Ukraine, came to America in 1872, studied English, and researched agricultural opportunities in the West. In 1873 he built a grist mill in Hal-stead; it was the first in Harvey County. The next year he helped five thousand Mennonite immigrants settle in Kansas.

Warkentin purchased the Monarch Mill in 1879 to mill the hard Turkey Red wheat. The Warkentins' home, now a museum, reflects the surprisingly opulent lifestyle of the affluent Mennonite entrepreneur. This Victorian home, with many original furnishings in place, opens a window into 1880s luxury. Note the leatherette wainscoting, red Russian carpets, oak doors with cut and etched glass from France, and crystal chandeliers from Czechoslovakia.

The legacy of Turkey Red wheat is still apparent in Newton and, for that matter, in the entire winter-wheat belt of the United States, because Turkey Red is the genetic base of most winter wheat. Prosperous farms with wheat as a major crop surround Newton. Grain elevators and a large modern flour mill attest to wheat's influence.

I was surprised at the number and diversity of shops on

Santa Fe steam locomotive number 1880

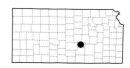

The home of pioneer miller Bernhard Warkentin

Newton's Main Street. There are fine clothing, shoes, furniture, hardware—all the stores you expect in a town of seventeen thousand—plus a host of unique shops and boutiques such as Charlotte's Sew Natural, with beautiful and unusual natural fabrics; Bradford Pear, an antique-inspired gift store with gourmet kitchen accessories, teas, cocoas, and coffees; Paper, Etc., which features gourmet foods as well as balloons, cards, and gifts; and the Good Earth General Store.

The nonprofit Et Cetera Shop is sponsored by Mennonite churches. There you can buy crafts and gifts made by needy people in thirty-five developing countries to support themselves. Items for sale include beautifully hand-carved Christmas scenes and animals—tigers, elephants, and more. Not far away is Anderson's Book and Office Supply, a five-generation family business over a hundred years old, selling almost everything. This venerable store, built in the 1880s, has original metal ceilings, fans, wood floors, and gas radiators.

Almost hidden on side streets are shops waiting to be discovered. High Street Company, in an old grocery store, will surprise you with its country atmosphere and the variety of gifts and antiques. On Broadway you'll find Memories in Miniature, a doll-house museum and shop. You'll be amazed at the collection of doll houses and miniatures showcased in a Victorian home. Also on Broadway is a delightful bakery, Dave's Delicacies, which features homemade breads, rolls, pies, and other goodies.

And this is only a small sample of the wonderful locally owned businesses you'll find when you explore Newton and other rural Kansas towns. You may strike up a conversation with the owner and receive personal attention and insight. It's fun to get acquainted with the people who are the backbone of rural America.

There are many choice restaurants in Newton. For ethnic cuisine the Breadbasket south of the old mill has few equals. The restaurant's German buffet menu, which includes verenika, whole-hog sausage, ham gravy, borscht, and cherry mos' makes my mouth water. For that special ambience try the Old Mill Restaurant and Bar. Downtown you'll find the cozy and delightful R J's Deli.

The Kauffman Museum on the Bethel College Campus is a must for the whole family. Outside you'll discover an actual pioneer farmstead and meander through a miniature prairie (the variety of flowers will astound you). Inside the story of the plains featuring the Mennonite migration is eloquently portrayed.

The list of Newton's attractions goes on: the Newton Station, modeled after Shakespeare's house at Stratford-upon-Avon; old steam locomotive number 1880 in the Military Park; 500 Main Place, an example of American Renaissance architecture and the home of the Newton Convention and Tourism Bureau; the Bethel College 1887 limestone Administration Building; and plaques detailing Newton history.

Five fine motels and two bed-and-breakfasts ensure a comfortable stay in Newton. Remember, Newton motels are only ten minutes from the Kansas Coliseum and Wichita Greyhound Park.

Peabody
Main Street Renaissance

In Peabody the buildings on Main Street visually communicate with you. They seem eager to tell their story. The massive early-frontier-style cornices draw your eyes to their beautiful new colors—pastel greens, pinks, yellows—and a host of textures. Most of the buildings display 1880s construction dates. New windows, recessed fronts, cast-iron columns, and restored front facades call out, "Look at me, I'm whole again." Through years of effort by Peabody's Main Street Association, downtown Peabody once more is a grand sight to behold, and furthermore all buildings are occupied by enthusiastic merchants.

I admired the structures, I photographed them, but something was missing. Finally I realized that the buildings were inviting me in, and what a revelation followed! The people within told me what the cleaned and repointed bricks and stones had been trying to say. I heard the stories of specific buildings, but they also tell the story of Kansas from the time when homesteaders and merchants followed the rails into the area. Peabody's buildings are tangible evidence of those pioneers' ambitions, successes, and lifestyles.

The chronicles of fires, an oil boom, the first highway, agriculture, and depressions are all recorded in brick and stone. I spent a fascinating day discovering the layers of history in these beautifully restored buildings. Let me tell you a few of the stories.

The Odd Fellows Hall was built in 1910 with the lower level being a garage to serve traffic on the New Santa Fe Auto Trail, now U.S. 50. It was advertised that you could leave your car here in the heated garage instead of draining the water on cold nights. Also responding to the new automobile culture, the Eyestone Building had a Ford Garage on the lower level and a Motor Inn Hotel on the second floor. During World War II German prisoners of war were quartered on the lower level with guards on the top level.

Phoenix Dry Goods, like the legendary bird that is its namesake, rose from ashes to become a modern clothing store. Six years ago a fire seriously damaged this 1884 store, but Steve Hamous carefully rebuilt using authentic fixtures and woodwork. A high corrugated wood ceiling (Peabody is the first town where I've seen corrugated wood used), the recessed front, skylights, and the wood floor are obvious old features, but it's details like the dressing rooms and clothing racks that tell the interesting stories.

A free-standing unit of four dressing rooms comes out of an old bank that during the oil boom days provided clean-up facilities in the basement for oil workers when they came into town on Saturday night. Now that was a full-service bank! The woodwork is excellent and the dressing rooms are larger than what modern stores offer. The

An example of Peabody's Main Street restoration

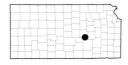

Customers and merchants relax on shaded benches

clothing racks are in wood closets with glass fronts. The clothes roll out on suspended tracks for the shoppers' viewing. Browse through Steve's selection of casual and work clothing as you recall an elegant era.

Steve said, "What you have here is so much better than new, and it's cheaper—limestone walls two feet thick—and the aura—the smell, the patina—is something you cannot replicate."

Retired teacher Gary Jones operates Mayesville Mercantile (if he's not sitting outside in the shade with friends) in an old restored grocery store. It's an appropriate place for an antique shop, but the store may be older than the antiques. Gary can tell you all about Peabody's Main Street Restoration program and the stories that go with each building.

Gary and his wife, Marilyn, also own the Jones Sheep Farm Bed-and-Breakfast. Its a small house in the country, no television or jacuzzi, but it offers rural country charm—flowers, grazing sheep, and serenity.

The Kansas State Fair came to Peabody in 1885. An octagonal building and the race track in the park are remnants of this event. A Peabody history book notes that Roman Chariot races were held and one driver was a woman. Peabody's park is a wonderful place for children; one resident left her entire estate to provide the large variety of playground equipment.

I have a question about the Peabody City Building on Main Street (please note that Main Street is officially called Walnut Street). Early pictures show this 1887 building with a tower on the southwest corner that makes it look much like the original city building in Kingman. The tower in the Kingman structure, circa 1888, was a fire hose drying tower. Is there a connection?

The Main Street Association's excellent brochure gives a brief historical synopsis of each building and describes the residential section of town as well. The style, size, and elegance of the old homes speak of prosperity and optimism. The brochure tells how W. M. Irwin came to Peabody in 1883, friendless and penniless, and sixteen years later built a sumptuous house that still looks grand.

The Queen Anne Cottage house of early Peabody newspaper publisher W. H. Morgan has been meticulously restored and furnished by the Peabody Historical Society. A matter of interest to me is the roof covering, called "terneplate," steel sheets covered with an alloy of tin and lead. The house seems stark without electric kitchen appliances, television, computer, and telephones. In the backyard are a barn and a flower garden.

Exploring the buildings of Peabody led me to one of my favorite subjects, food. The dominant building in town, limestone walls and spires set over the cornices, is now Sharon's Kountry Kitchen. You'll find good food and a great place for talk of the town at breakfast and lunch. At the other end of town the Turkey Red Restaurant has recently opened in Peabody's original post office. I may have to come back here often because on Fridays and Saturdays they feature an "Around the World" menu—a different country's cuisine every two weeks. I could get to know the flavors of twenty-six countries in one year.

Pittsburg

Doodah Day! Fifty-Four Scrumptious Places to Eat

Camptown Races—oh, doodah day! Romance clings to the name Camptown, the pulse accelerates, flags fly, and crowds cheer, but where does the name Camptown come from? I set out to explore this magic word in Pittsburg and Crawford County.

I soon discovered that the word Camptown literally and historically has great meaning in Crawford County. I found Arma, Camp 50, Frontenac, Weir, Cherokee, Roseland, Scammon, all camp towns—coal mining camp towns. Between 1880 and 1940 more than thirty-one thousand people from southern and eastern Europe came to Crawford County to work in the coal fields, and Crawford and Cherokee counties became known as the Little Balkans.

What a bittersweet story! The human drama here moves from blackest despair to joyous ethnic festivities and cuisine. I've talked with miners who endured black hell a hundred feet below the ground, and I've heard about good times—Italians playing Bocci ball, English running foot races, Germans and Austrians dancing the polka.

There is a diorama in the Crawford County Museum you must see to understand the pathos of the camp town. It depicts a grimy, stooped miner laboring in a black coal vein. The thought of working long days in a dusty tunnel four feet high illuminated only by a miner's lamp, pushing and kicking coal back with hands and feet, makes me shudder. The museum also tells of community progress and the fight for workers' rights; it relates the Little Balkans story, and it explains the strip mines.

Even before the Civil War, settlers came to farm the rolling prairies, but that all changed with the discovery of coal. As the coal industry developed, vast fortunes were made, immigrants were exploited, and the land itself was altered to the point where an early settler wouldn't recognize it today. Early coal mines were shaft mines, but, with the advent of the huge power shovel, strip mining came to Crawford County.

It takes the fortitude of an old-time explorer to envision the immenseness and grasp the impact of strip mining on the land, the people, and the present potential of this area. I studied maps; talked to Stan Harter, the area wildlife manager; drove many miles; and tramped through thickets and vines to get the picture. I learned that thousands and thousands of acres of prairie had been literally plowed, some sixty feet deep, by power shovels weighing as much as eleven-million pounds, and then the land was abandoned, a jumble of mixed soils, pits, and ridges.

It might have been an environmental catastrophe, but nature's resilience and human ingenuity changed this man-made devastation into a luxuriant wilderness bountiful with game and fish.

It took my new Kansas-exploring eyes a while to see how beauty had been superimposed on top of chaos. A morning walk in Mined Land Wildlife Area Number One just north of Frontenac opened my new explorer eyes wide. A great blue heron rose ponderously out of a morning mist, and snapping turtles basked on slimy logs. The surrounding foliage was lush green except for a catalpa flowering white. Gilded streaks momentarily followed a flock of cavorting goldfinches across the still waters. A flicker calling, a squirrel's bark, and the harsh tones of a bullfrog added sound effects to the morning show.

Of course, the black gold bonanza affected more than the land. In the Little Balkans of Kansas, coal miners represented fifty-two nationalities. They had fled oppression and poverty in

Fishing is great in the strip-mined pits

Europe, and they angrily resisted it here. When union busters came to the coal fields, defiant women marched in the "Amazon Army." A socialist newspaper, the *Appeal to Reason*, advocated workers' rights, the forty-hour work week, equality for women, and fair child-labor practices. In 1913 the circulation of this newspaper, published in Girard, the Crawford County seat, was the largest in the world. And while most Kansans were proud of Carrie Nation's bar-bashing campaign, the people of the Little Balkans with their diversity of languages, social mores, and fierce quest for independence made a shambles of prohibition.

Harold Bell Wright, author of *The Shepherd of the Hills*, came to Pittsburg in 1898 as minister of the First Christian Church. His experience with injustice and vice rampant in Pittsburg influenced him to write his first novel, *That Printer of Udell's*, based on a series of his sermons dealing with everyday life in Pittsburg. He was the first American author to earn a million dollars from his writing.

How should you experience Pittsburg? I suggest three E's on your first visit there: exploring, eating, and entertainment. Explore the city: the mysterious stone faces, Hotel Stilwell (I suggest breakfast in Otto's Cafe, which is part of the hotel), Wright's home, the college campus, and a bookstore that loves books (Mostly Books).

Explore Girard, which offers a wonderful drive-by tour (one-half mile east on K-57 you'll see one of the largest flags in the nation, 30 by 60 feet, flying 130 feet high). You'll discover a heartwarming story and sight west of Girard at Greenbush. You'll see the ruins of a stone church destroyed by fire in 1982, beautiful even now, and nearby a circa 1881 church that was restored to replace the newer structure. At Frontenac follow the aroma of Italian and French breads to the old-fashioned bakery. Explore the mined lands and the camp towns.

I counted fifty-four places to eat in Pittsburg alone, but what is really great is the diversity of cuisine. Recipes from the old country make your mouth water. You must get involved in the chicken wars—Chicken Annie's and Chicken Mary's have been dishing it out for years. It's up to you to pick the winner. It's difficult to choose; one has a bigger sign, the other is a block closer to the highway, one has a windmill, the other has a red roof and brick facade—the food is great in both.

Where to stay? Motels abound in every price range, and there are campgrounds from full service to primitive.

I've barely touched on what you can do here to enjoy a day or two, a week. . . or maybe you'll just want to call it home.

Pratt

Home of the Miss Kansas Pageant

Pratt, Kansas, might well be the quintessential Main Street U.S.A. city of the nineties. A feeling of home pervades its tree-lined brick streets. Charming shops, cozy cafes, and an art-deco theater grace the main thoroughfare. At the same time the wheels and bytes of commerce are energetically moving Pratt into the twenty-first century. It seems the perfect place for Miss Kansas and, yes, even Miss America, to make an entrance.

An old tree carved into a beautiful eagle

I visited Pratt as an official explorer for the Kansas Explorers' Club, so I viewed the city in the context of the club's list of rural culture elements: geography, history, architecture, commerce, customs, art, cuisine, and people.

Geography, which includes flora and fauna, was easy. A great blue heron, posturing in a marsh among some cattails, was in easy camera range as I drove through the wetlands at the Kansas Wildlife and Parks headquarters. A car makes an ideal blind in areas like this where auto paths snuggle up to the wildscape. In the Wildlife Museum and Aquarium near the headquarters, prairie dioramas, live reptile displays, and native fish swimming bring Kansas nature lore to children and adults throughout the year, regardless of the weather.

A nature trail meandering through a wooded area is new in Lemon Park, one of eighteen parks in Pratt offering a variety of picnicking, sports, swimming, bird-watching, and relaxation. West of Pratt the Texas Lake Wildlife Area and the Pratt Sandhills Wildlife Area provide upland game and waterfowl hunting opportunities.

For a nostalgic walk down a bygone small-town Main Street, I visited the Pratt County Historical Museum. This is not one of those musty places where shabby stuffed owls, mangy buffalo robes, and pictures of someone else's great-great-grandfather abound. Remember the old-fashioned lumberyard with driveways between open lumber sheds? Imagine all this under one roof with life-size Main Street business replicas replacing the lumber on either side of the driveways. A boardwalk connects a general store, a butcher shop, a tonsorial parlor featuring hot baths, a livery stable complete with tack room, and much more. In other galleries are a blacksmith shop, a firehouse, and an auto repair shop, plus exquisite wood miniatures, the

railroad room, and much more to evoke the days of long ago.

Wheat, oil, and cattle drive the economy in Pratt County. In fact, the nation's largest independent livestock sale barn is just a few miles east of town. It's sale day when you see the huge cattle semis and ranch pickups parked there. Stop in and feel the drama as the auctioneer's chant and a buyer's casual nod send thousands of pounds of living beef to your meat market. You'll gain a new appreciation for the unique breed of people who produce those delicious steaks and hamburgers. Speaking of hamburgers, you can get a tasty one and enjoy the '57 Chevy decor at

Phil's 54 Diner on Highway 54.

Pratt combines the best of two worlds—the good old days and modern comforts. U.S. 54 running through town caters to modern America on wheels, while Main Street provides everything from clothing stores to avant-garde coffee shops. Gracious homes south of town blend into the rolling terrain, while elsewhere contemporary subdivisions are growing. Good schools, a junior college, a medical center, twenty-three churches, theaters, and many parks make Pratt feel like home.

What is this magic that can blend old-fashioned pioneer values and traditions with the best of the nineties? As in many other communities, it appears to be a spirit of volunteerism, initiative, and courage reviving in Kansas.

Dorotha Giannangelo, Pratt

Believe it or not, hot and cold water towers

County Historical Museum's curator, told me, "We planned a Pratt volunteer appreciation day. When the list was completed there were more than eight hundred names. Isn't that great for a town of seven thousand!"

Downtown the old storefronts are still there, refurbished and well kept, but inside, merchants are adapting to competition from the new superstores with extra service, innovative products, sophisticated marketing, and competitive prices.

Pat Lickiss at the Main Street Antiques Mall says, "Eighty percent of our business is out-of-town traffic, and half of that is out-of-state. Antique shops bring a lot of business to town."

"It's a slower pace here. You get to know the people," says John Martin, owner of the Coffee Trader. John and his wife, Michele, recent emigrants from California, feature gourmet coffee and tea by the pound, espresso machines, creative cookware, and table settings, and in the deli they serve delicious sandwiches, exotic pies, and specialties such as Italian sodas and banana gorillas.

Raised in Bavaria, Trudy Smith works at Peggy's, a jewelry and gift shop.

"At first Kansas shocked me," Trudy says. "The beauty of the landscape in Bavaria hits you, but Kansas is more subtle...the majesty of space...the changing colors—I like Kansas now."

The inviting avenue of trees and park benches along Main Street clearly says, "Stop by and visit a spell."

I've made numerous trips to Lemon Park and it's always lovely. Recently a winding and not at all obtrusive concrete walking trail a mile in length has been added. Always there are enthusiastic walkers, young and old, fast and slow— couples, a man with a dog—breathing in the clean air and absorbing the ever-changing beauty of this wooded paradise. I watched a young mother pushing a stroller at a most amazing speed while a friend ran breathlessly beside her. The little one in the stroller was enjoying every moment. I'm sure my little granddaughters would love the brightly colored slides, tunnels, and swings in the playground.

Chain-saw art attracts me; it seems such an unlikely mixture of strength and softness. How such a noisy, smelly machine that cuts down huge trees can, with its master, create a coyote, an owl, a raccoon, or a boy and his dog perplexes me even though I like to run a chain saw myself. Lemon Park and the Outdoor Wildlife Learning Site at the Southwest Elementary School host this unusual menagerie. But the best specimen is an eagle atop an American flag at the courthouse.

Enjoy Pratt. I did.

Rawlins County
Life Beyond the Fast Lane

Rawlins County and Atwood, its county seat, are an explorer's delight. There is an ambience about the town that subtly speaks of mystery tempered with charm and a reasonable bustle of commerce. It's as if someone had planted a storybook village on the plains of Kansas. I set out to discover why local people and visitors like this out-of-the-way town so much, and you'll enjoy doing the same.

Atwood is a surprise when you come upon it; it is literally hidden in the Beaver Creek Valley. Once down in the valley, travelers at the intersection of U.S. 36 and K-25 perceive towering cottonwoods and the blue waters of Lake Atwood.

Entering Atwood on a very hot day I was drawn from the highway by a cool lane—cottonwoods forming an overhead canopy—winding around the lake. The first thing I noticed was a sign proclaiming that Horace Greeley, founder of the *New York Tribune*, came through the area on a Pike's Peak Express stagecoach in 1859. Indians spooked the mules and upset the stage. Greeley was rescued "and taken to station 17 ... where the good woman dressed his galling wounds." (See "Wallace County" elsewhere in this book for another perspective on the story.)

Down the lane I passed a covered walking bridge under the shade of more giant cottonwoods. I love those trees—the way their leaves shimmer and softly rustle in a slight breeze. I'll always remember Atwood for its profusion of cottonwoods. Underneath the trees I noticed a hiking path that circles the lake. The shaded campsites and picnic areas looked inviting.

At the far reach of the lake the Ol' Depot Shop beckoned me. The depot itself is a large, two-story structure built by the Burlington Northern in 1889. Inside, thirty local crafters and collectible and antique dealers display their wares.

Coming into town on U.S. 36 you might think that it is Atwood's main street, but Main Street is actually six blocks south of the highway. Maybe it's the space between that preserves the provincial aura, "provincial" in the best sense of the word: authentic and unspoiled. Some streets have median islands planted with trees and flowers and are illuminated with old-fashioned street lamps. The 1907 Romanesque Revival courthouse on the east end of Main Street, a Pete Felten buffalo statue in the middle of the street, and a nearby bed-and-breakfast with a profusion of flowers and

Mural in the Rawlins County Museum

herbs add to the town's charm.

In the Rawlins County Historical Museum a huge mural by Rudolph Wendelin, famous as the Smokey the Bear artist for fifty years, depicts the Rawlins County mystique. Emphasized in this large collage are vignettes of the history that made the community. Notice the look of courageous confidence on the face of a man leading a covered wagon. The general store in the museum is a gem. From the spools of multicolored thread in a rack to a machine for selecting your eyeglasses, everything is authentic. An unusually large collection of authentic Kachina dolls (Hopi Indian ceremonial dolls made out of cottonwood roots) is also on display here.

Find time to talk to Craig Cox, the museum curator. He knows the territory and will help you plan your exploration. He observed to me that the rough terrain in Rawlins County contributes to the pastoral image. Farms are cut up by the many branches of Beaver and Sappa creeks, leaving grassland strips, so almost every farm has some cattle to utilize the grass (an unusual practice in most of Kansas).

I visited with Arlene Bliss, head of the Rawlins County Economic Development Association. She told me about the community spirit that empowers the town and county. She explained how

Debra Johnson in her McDonald Grocery Store

the community rallied behind constructing Lake Atwood, moving an old church into town, and restoring the Jayhawk Theater, all basically accomplished with private funds and local effort. Standing near the museum is an old country church that closed its doors in 1979. The parishioners lovingly maintained it in mint condition until the community at large raised the money to move it fifteen miles into town—steeple and all. Today it is part of the historical complex that reflects the community's faith and vision. The theater's marquee once again is lit up announcing movies and local stage productions.

The Rawlins County Historical Museum has county maps available that detail intriguing points of interest in Rawlins County, including old townsites, stone houses, the first homestead, opaline cliffs, and various caves. One cave in particular, Belle Starr's Cave, caught my attention. Arlene was flabbergasted that I had never heard of Belle Starr, the notorious female

outlaw of the 1800s. Quite sure that Belle would be docile by now, I went searching for the cave. I found some checkpoints, the town site of Achilles (only a schoolhouse remains), and the Sappa Creek loop that crosses the road, but I didn't find the cave. I suggest you ask for help in the neighborhood.

Many towns on the map are mostly memories, but some, like McDonald (population 179) are good places to visit. Stop in at Brenda Johnson's old-fashioned grocery store. Really, they have everything you need, and watch Brenda smile when she rings up your purchase on the cash register. Across the street the Frosty Mug is a great place to soak up some western atmosphere as you enjoy their famous lunch or dinner.

On the other side of the county I met a character I want you to meet. In Herndon stop in at Pooch's Pizza, order a sandwich or pizza, and strike up a conversation with Harold. That man makes the Rawlins County hills come alive with his stories: "Why, I remember the last major dust storm in April 1940; the sky was black...then it rained...it was over." He told me to invite you.

I suggest that you give yourself time for relaxation, call Arlene for some information, check into an Atwood bed-and-breakfast or local motel, and explore Rawlins County.

Stockton

Bittersweet Memories and Courageous Living

I knew I'd love Stockton as soon as I saw the old threshers and tractors on the south end of town. Now my wife might be the one to say, "What's all that junk doing there?" but I take great pleasure in seeing old farm machinery in its natural state, rusty but ready to go.

Stockton is the home of the famous Solomon Valley Antique Engine and Machinery Association and its annual show in late September. Of course, there's much more to Stockton then relic farm tractors, but the antique equipment symbolizes an appreciation of old roots and solid values that makes Stockton a great place to live... and to visit.

Take Smith's Furniture Company. I don't think John and Roma would mind my telling you that they're senior, senior citizens who have spent a good part of their life together traveling in more than forty countries. They've purchased fine new reproductions of classic gift items, decoration accessories, cut glass, and furniture. Discriminating gift shoppers come from many states for a unique and sophisticated selection.

I could very easily settle into a comfortable routine here in Stockton: breakfast at the K & V Cafe (watch the town wake up), journey to Nicodemus and Webster Lake, lunch at Cindy Lou's (local friends say bring a newspaper), tour the museum, see the log hotel, go for a country drive, check out Woodston, have sup-per at the Country Inn (windup of farmer weather talk)... check in at Midwest Motel (I did because Chuck has an antique tractor parked there). Next day same routine with different

places to explore and shop... try supper in Damar at the Country Folks Restaurant for prime rib, crab legs, and lamb fries (ask for lamb fry info *after* supper).

As you travel west on K-4 you'll see layers of massive rocks in road cuts appearing to have been laid by a mason of Paul Bunyan's stature. These unique strata of limestone are known as the Fort Hays Formation. You may have encountered the post rock strata farther east in Kansas, and layers of red sandstone beyond. I'm discovering that as you travel from east to west in Kansas you're gradually climbing more than three thousand feet and that each change in elevation reveals new formations of base material. The next layer up, which you can see in Rooks County, is chalky lime-

Threshing machine in outdoor display, Stockton

stone similar to that which makes up the Chalk Pyramids.

At a point about three miles west of Stockton, where the road curves south, you can see a cave eroded into a rock wall. When I arrived the morning light was streaming into the little cave, so I stopped for a quick photo. I imagined there must be a story of pioneer days here, perhaps a homesteader finding temporary shelter.

Farther west I came upon a cluster of houses that appeared to be a town without any visible main street. A sign said, "Welcome to Nicodemus" and explained that black settlers from Kentucky founded Nicodemus in 1877. Today it's the only remaining black settlement west of the Mississippi River. Angela Bates, local historian and information resource, is seeking to establish Nicodemus as a National Historic Place. Bittersweet memories and courageous living are commemorated annually at the Nicodemus Emancipation Celebration in late July. You are welcome in Nicodemus, where a number of residences, a community center, and a church remain.

In Nicodemus I learned more about the cave west of Stockton. Sadly, at one time black people were not permitted to stay overnight in Stockton (which, of course, was not unique in this practice). When Nicodemus citizens went shop-

The public library in Stockton

ping for supplies in Stockton, the little cave was their overnight home.

I was still thinking about the effect of cultural differences when I drove into Damar. This little town (population 112) is dominated by the St. Joseph's Church, a beautiful romanesque twin-tower structure built in increments from 1913 to 1952 by local labor. I tried the door; it was locked. Someone shouted from across the street, "Try the other door." I was glad he did; the inside was a tribute to humankind's quest for beauty.

An old-country atmosphere clings to Damar's short main street. As you may have guessed by now, I'm eating my way across the state, so I walked into the Country Folks Family Restaurant. Honestly, I tried to pass by the pies, but I succumbed to the coconut cream pie. It was great, and I learned a lot about the community from Leona Newell, the restaurants owner. She told me that Damar had been settled by French farmers in the 1880s and that,

as is true of many other ethnic communities, the old ways and language are disappearing. She also talked of French dough fried bread served with syrup, and of delicious lacy crepes.

Outside once more, I saw the main street with new eyes. The French influence was obvious—white buildings subtly different in shape and roof line from Yankee and German architecture.

If you're interested in early Kansas architecture, a Stockton Heritage Walking Tour arranged by Leo Oliva is very informative. I find that whether I'm bird-watching or house-looking, identification by name makes it more meaningful. Oliva's brochure allows you to match up terminology with actual houses—mansard roof, vernacular center gable, Queen Anne, bungalow, and so forth.

The exhibits were not quite complete in the new Rooks County Historical Museum when I visited it in the summer of 1995, but I was impressed with what I saw. Well-designed booths display vignettes of Rooks County pioneer life. By the way, do you know what a Crosley ice ball is? See one in the museum here.

Allow yourself the time to leisurely roam the white stone byways of Rooks County. Rub shoulders with the people; take an interest in their lives; visit the little towns. Allow what is there to tell you its story.

WaKeeney

Stagecoaches, Timber Claims, and Tigers

Allen Wild is a man of action. Never having met him before, I was surprised when he said, "Get in my old Scout and I'll show you." Just as Allen put the pickup in gear, a collie barreled through the driver's open window, ending up beside me. What a ride it was, pushing through grasses taller than the pickup, scaring deer, and bouncing through a creek.

When I met Allen, I was exploring traces of the Smoky Hill Trail and the short-lived Butterfield and Overland Dispatch Stagecoach route in Trego County south of WaKeeney. The Smoky Hill Trail was the shortest route to the gold fields in Colorado, but it was known as the Trail of Death because of Indian problems and lack of water at times. Allen knew exactly where to drive in the rugged Smoky Hill breaks to find elusive landmarks.

"There, see where the grass is a little darker? That's where the Ruthdon campsite was."

We continued on west toward Wildcat Canyon. Allen pointed out B.O.D. markers on roadsides and sometimes faint traces of the trail. Often, on high points, we could glimpse Castle Rock still several miles west.

The Smoky Hill Trail is a place where events popularized by movie Westerns—a stagecoach racing pell-mell over rough trails, Indians attacking, and the U.S. Cavalry charging to the rescue—occurred in true life. Key points on the Smoky Hill trail, such as Threshing Machine Canyon, Stormy Hollow, Downer's Station, and Ruthdon, are the raw material of Hollywood drama. It all happened here in Kansas, especially Trego County.

Did all the adventure and excitement in WaKeeney end a hundred years ago? As I was talking history with Jim Cleland in his pharmacy and gift shop, an attractive young lady walked in with a baby—a baby Bengal tiger. One roar from "Tiga" and she had everybody's attention. The ladies at the old-fashioned soda fountain just about dropped their spoons. Tiga's "mom" put her down and let her explore. Even at thirteen weeks a Bengal tiger is a force to reckon with. Jim introduced me to Toni Pfeifer and a contemporary adventure.

Toni buys and sells tigers, bears, and other animals and she also trains and stables horses. That afternoon I went to Cottonwood Hollow Stables to see her most unusual business. As I arrived Toni was feeding a little beaver, just old enough to open its eyes. She will accept orphaned or injured wild animals, but, she explained, wild animals must be returned to their natural habitats and released as soon as possible. You cannot keep them as pets or sell them. We walked out to the tiger pens she was building, fashioned out of heavy steel oilfield tanks (her husband Terry operates an oilfield dozer service).

"I just bought two Siberian tigers and I must get the pens approved by state and federal inspectors before I can bring the tigers home," she said, adding, "over there is the bear's house. I traded two wildcats for him."

Momentarily a masculine bias crossed my mind, and I thought, "How could this petite girl dream of handling those large animals?"

She read my mind and said, "It's not physical force but poise and confidence that control."

Toni and Terry's ranch was homesteaded as a timber claim in 1894 (a percentage of land was planted to trees to claim the tract). Rows of stately cottonwoods are still there to shade deer, tigers, bears, and (coming soon) a dry-land hippo.

Back to WaKeeney. At the town's two I-70 exits are comfortable service stations, motels, and the usual variety of fast-food restaurants. While proximity to I-70

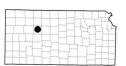

Castle Rock near WaKeeney

offers commercial advantages, WaKeeney manages to preserve its own farm-and-ranch-country identity. Its main street is attractive and thriving, and except for an occasional tiger in town it is secure and comfortable. It's the type of town where people like to raise their children and eventually retire.

During the Christmas season Main Street turns into a Christmas fantasy land. A festive tradition, started in 1955, begins with inspired citizens, two tons of pine boughs, a forty-foot pole, six thousand bulbs, and

miles of wire. Lights stretched from the Christmas tree to decorated sidewalk posts form a colorful canopy under the winter sky. What family fun—hot chocolate, wagon rides, shopping, and Christmas carols. I suspect the true spirit of Christmas resides in WaKeeney.

Meanwhile Jim Cleland had good news for me and quite possibly for you, dear reader. Following our tiger-interrupted conversation he had made a few phone calls and had lunch discussions about the *Exploring*

Kansas project. He said farmers and businessmen had volunteered to let visitors ride with them while working to experience life on the farm, a livestock auction, and the Smoky Hill River Valley's historical, scenic, and hunting attractions. Imagine riding with a farmer in his pickup while he checks cattle or irrigation systems, fuels tractors, or hauls wheat. If you have no farming experience I guarantee you'll shatter a few stereotypical images of farm life. Check with Jim Cleland or Kerry Benisch for arrangements.

For the night my destination was Thistle Hill Bed-and-Breakfast, owned by David and Mary Hendricks. With an hour of sunlight left I looped around to Castle Rock and the Badlands. Only twenty miles from I-70 this lone pinnacle, like a specter from an ancient world, speaks to the soul about the awesome reality of time and the transitory nature of our lives. Paradoxically I realized I was late and must rush.

Into the approaching darkness I raced on rocky, unfamiliar roads around the Badlands, by Wildcat Canyon, cautioned by deer on the road, to Thistle Hill.

David's first remark when he greeted me was, "Your tire is going flat."

The peaceful charm of this prairie inn enfolded me, and soon I was dreaming of tigers chasing stagecoaches.

Wallace County
Mountain Climbing in Western Kansas

Wow! What a day! What a trip! Mind you, I went mountain climbing, explored Hell's Half Acre, peeked into a haunted house, and finally traipsed through a graveyard with my two special guides— a rattlesnake lady and a very, very pregnant Chamber of Commerce director.

Probably not your typical day in Kansas, but in Wallace County anything can happen: In 1926 the earth opened up near the Smoky Hill River, leaving a crater four hundred fifty feet across and one hundred seventy feet deep. A writer for the *St. Louis Post Dispatch* noted that "... for this community [Wallace] of 1,000 this hole is a yawning abyss, deep and threatening—and profitable." Soon after, stock was issued in the Smoky Basin Oil and Gas Company.

In the old Fort Wallace Cemetery is the grave of a man shotgunned to death. Next to him lies his assailant, hanged by the county a few months later.

More recently, at the local golf course after a golfer hit an unusually long drive, his elation turned to astonishment as a prairie swift fox bolted across the fairway, grabbed the ball, and disappeared in the sagebrush.

I met Lisa Walker, the Chamber of Commerce director, and Judie Withers, Rattlesnake Roundup promoter, in Sharon Springs. As we headed for the city park Lisa told me about their unusual annual carnival in July. With the versatility common among rural people, they build and operate their own carnival rides and concession stands. Why? For financial, safety, and security reasons. Lisa said, "One little girl gave the carny operator her purse to hold while she took a ride."

Simple but eloquent monument on Mount Sunflower

Judie spoke up. "See that building over there? That's where we have the rattlesnake pit during the Rattlesnake Roundup. We dump about three hundred rattlers in there, then the handlers get in there, and...." She went on to tell me about a local lady who invites rattlers into her sleeping bag during the show. Roundup activities include a ham-and-bean feed, crafters, a rattlesnake lunch, and a variety of entertainment.

How do you top that? By climbing to the top of Mount Sunflower, the highest point in Kansas at an elevation of 4,039 feet. Don't expect snow-capped peaks (you can find them in nearby Colorado anytime), but do anticipate the ever-changing grandeur of the High Plains—the song of a lark bunting, the splendor of the Shortgrass Prairie grasses and delicate flowers, and a kaleidoscopic sky—brilliant dawns of every hue, azure mornings, blazing white summer heat, and the gray of a gentle spring rain. Let your new Kansas explorer eyes gaze with wonder on the miles and miles of rolling plains and the endless circle of the far horizon. A simple yet eloquent welded steel sunflower, created by Ed Harold, stands at the high point facing the Kansas sunrise every morning.

Twenty years of early Wallace County history encapsulate the

Original 1866 stagecoach station

real drama movie and television westerns are made of—Indian wars, stagecoaches, railroad builders, and trail cowboys. Native Americans, of course, were in what is now Wallace County long before George Custer and his contemporaries arrived in the area (evidences of Native American culture in this area date back two thousand years). A string of U.S. military forts followed the white incursion into the West. Fort Wallace, near present-day Wallace, was established in 1865 to protect the Smoky Hill Trail, the Butterfield Overland Dispatch stage line (1865 to 1866), and the westward-reaching railroads of the late 1860s. The town of Wallace became a Kansas Pacific Railroad division point when the tracks reached there in 1869. The coming of the railroads to Kansas ended the era of stagecoach and covered-wagon trails and ushered in the cowboy trails trampled by longhorn cattle from Texas.

With good new explorer eyes it's still possible to recreate the rough-and-tumble Wallace County golden days. In the 1880s the town of Wallace had a population of thirty-five hundred. Today it is seventy-five. The original Pond Creek Station, built in 1865 as a home station for the Butterfield Overland Dispatch, has been moved to the site of the Fort Wallace Historical Museum near Wallace. This old station, miscellaneous wagons and a cannon, a nearby Weskan Depot, and countless artifacts and documents in the museum are the raw material that a vivid imagination can convert to the virtual reality of the late 1800s.

A curious story about Horace Greeley is told and documented in the museum. It's said that Greeley, founder of the *New York Tribune*, came through the area on a stagecoach in the 1860s. His coach horses were spooked by Indians and the coach upset near Pond Creek Station.

Greeley is quoted as saying, "The woman there took good care of me [after the accident]." Oddly, the same story is told verbatim in another county. Poor Horace; it must have been a rough trip.

I never did see any ghosts, but there are surely some in Wallace, where at one time cavalrymen, gandy dancers, cowboys, and dance hall girls whooped it up. (Some of their extravagances are documented on wooden markers in the Fort Wallace Cemetery.) A Kansas Pacific limestone section house, circa 1879, sits forlorn in the weeds. A house built a year later, hiding behind a cloak of trees, seemed to harbor something mysterious. This once-proud Gothic Revival-style house was the home of Peter Robidoux, an entrepreneur who claimed to be a dealer in everything. Neighbors say a light occasionally glows in the kitchen.

To gain a perspective of what Horace Greeley, the cavalrymen, and early settlers encountered, you must drive out into the rangeland. Walk into a pasture until your car, the road, and the fences are out of sight. Stand in the wild grasses; embrace the wind, whether it be hot or cold; sense the presence of hostile faces on the other side of the hill; stoop to feel the soil, and ask yourself, as the settlers did, "Does this feel like home?"

The Kansas Sampler Festival

First full weekend of every October, Penner Farm, Inman, Kansas, 3 miles south, 1 ¾ miles east of Inman on Arapaho Road

Hi. I'm Marci Penner, executive director of the Kansas Sampler Foundation and Milferd's daughter. I've traveled the state quite a bit, but reading Dad's book makes me anxious to get on the road again and fine-tune my own explorations of Kansas. Just to give you a little more incentive to travel Kansas I'd like to invite you to the annual Kansas Sampler Festival. This is the place to rub shoulders with others who love exploring Kansas and with communities that put out the welcome mat!

This annual celebration now attracts more than 120 communities to the Penner Farm to offer a sample of what there is to see and do in Kansas. The idea is to encourage people to think about taking Kansas day trips and travel on the backroads and blue highways of Kansas.

The event started in 1990 as a small book-signing party for the first *Kansas Weekend Guide*. We never dreamed what would happen, but the event has blossomed into a full-fledged, statewide, sixteen port-a-pot festival. Last year seventy people signed on to help organize this event. They are now known as the very dedicated and hospitable Team Sampler.

The Sampler Festival hosts many colorful dance groups

At the festival, communities remind visitors of the specialness of rural communities. They set up exhibit booths in large tents, perform stage acts on the grassed-earthen stage bordered by Mom's flowers, tell stories, do character portrayals, show videos, and present slide shows in our barnlike Kansas Sampler Center. They do some proud orating about what their community has to offer on the famous "stump."

This working farm has been converted into a beautiful place in the country with fifty-one varieties of trees and shrubs, flower gardens, a pond, a two-acre prairie with trails, a tree-lined creek (site of the Cave Trail), and several outbuildings. I sometimes

Ethnic and Kansas specialty foods are always popular

Willis Loganbill provides carriage rides at the festival

rocks, buffalo burgers, and enchiladas.

People love to stroll the fourteen acres and enjoy the music on the deck of the pond, take the surrey rides through the shelter belt, and shuffle through the autumn leaves in the Cave Trail.

This event is created and produced by those who have a passion for rural community life. We invite you to attend the celebration and discover all that Kansas has to offer.

The Kansas Sampler Festival is a project of the Kansas Sampler Foundation. Call 316-585-2374 for more information.

wonder what my great-great-grandfather, who settled this farm in 1874, would think of all this. We now use the alfalfa field as a parking lot, the grain elevator houses art exhibits, and the old wood shed serves as a backdrop for the bierock vendor. The former sheep pasture is filled with exhibit tents, llama pens, and strolling minstrels.

The festival is designed as a fun but educational tool to tell the rural culture story of Kansas communities—including the cuisine. No hamburgers or hot dogs are allowed at the festival. All the food (cuisine) booths must consist of ethnic or specialty foods. Some of the favorite annual food booths are those that serve verenika, bie-

Kansas performers provide continuous shows under tents

The Kansas Explorers Club

Marci Penner

A brainstorming session at a retreat for rural community leaders led to the creation of the inimitable Kansas Explorers Club. The club was designed to be fun, to help people see Kansas with new eyes, and to recognize exploring and searching for the subtle beauty of Kansas as a valued activity.

By Kansas Day 1996, the end of its charter year, the club had attracted 418 members. It continues to grow. Each member receives a membership card, an explorer number, and a bimonthly newsletter—and learns the secret explorers' ritual.

The *Explorer* newsletter teaches the art of exploring and shares information about what can be found in the nooks and crannies

Kansas Explorers, the Susie and the LuWonda team

of the state. It tells about such important things as where to find the most delicious homemade pie and the best chicken-fried steak. Explorers share information about old-fashioned soda fountains, scenic drives, peaceful hiking trails, and whatever else stirs their fancy.

One of the first things an explorer learns is the rural culture elements: history, architecture, geography, commerce, cuisine, customs, art, and people. Dad has used the rural culture elements throughout his new book, *Exploring Kansas*. Looking for these elements makes it easy to discover the story of a town. In fact, the most fascinating way to explore is to see how the elements differ from town to town, region

Far horizons challenge the Kansas explorer

to region. Explorers learn to note architectural similarities and differences in neighboring communities; observe how the soil changes among geologic regions; and discover the major form of commerce, past and present, in a certain area.

Above all else, exploring should be fun! Fun is the reason that ace explorers Susie and the LuWondas have become famous for their uplifting manner of describing their Kansas adventures through song, dance, and costume. Fun is one reason we have Kansas Explorer Club trips. Fun is one reason the membership fee is $18.61 (the year Kansas became a state)!

Explorers Murray and Alyssa Penner visit Serenata Farms

Marci Penner exploring Old Albany

Explorers even find it fun to spend money in small towns!

Explorers learn to enjoy Kansas and the search for the nuances and the diversity. They learn to take time—to put their feet in a clear, cool stream, to lie down in the Flint Hills and watch the clouds go by, or to walk barefooted on a sandy road in the Arkansas River Lowlands. Explorers find much to enjoy about Kansas.

We hope that the Kansas Explorers Club will help people feel prouder of Kansas and make a difference in helping keep rural communities alive and thriving.

The Kansas Explorers Club is a project of the Kansas Sampler Foundation.

Travel Information

Below are telephone numbers for most of the people and places in *Exploring Kansas*. The first entry under each community generally has brochures and other information about food, lodging, and attractions. Call during business hours. Try the other phone numbers on weekends and evenings, and for details about specific attractions.

The businesses, attractions, and services in this book represent just a few of each community's many fine establishments. It was not possible to visit them all—so there are many exciting discoveries yet to be made.

ABILENE
1990 population 6,242
1970 population 6,661
Abilene Visitor Center, Pat McKee, 800-569-5915 or 913-263-2231
Abilene and Smoky Valley Railroad, 913-263-1077
Dickinson County Heritage Center, 913-263-2681
Eisenhower Center, 913-363-4751
Great Plains Theater, 913-263-4574
Kirby House, 913-263-7336
Lebold-Vahsholtz Mansion, 913-263-4356
Seelye Mansion, 913-263-1084

ASHLAND
1990 population 1,032
1970 population 1,244
Pioneer Museum, Floretta Rogers, 316-635-2227
Airport, Tod or Jo Peterson, 316-635-4055
Lodging: Debra Fox, Ashland City Hall, 316-635-2531

Rolling Hills Bed and Breakfast, Essie Waits, 316-635-2859
Scenic and wildflower information, Phil Arnold, 316-635-4071

ATCHISON
1990 population 10,656
1970 population 12,565
Atchison Chamber of Commerce, 800-234-1854 or 913-367-2427
Cray Historical Museum, 913-367-3046
Drury Pennell House, 913-367-4996
Haderway Tea Room, rural Lancaster, Connie Emory, 913-874-5771
Paolucci's Restaurant, 913-367-6105
This Ol' House, rural Nortonville, June Friend, 913-886-6685
Woolly Meadows, rural Nortonville, Harold and Carol Spencer, 913-886-2733

BUHLER
1990 population 1,277
1970 population 1,019
Buhler Chamber of Commerce at Buhler Agency, Leon Kliewer, 800-397-3072 or 316-543-2244
Adrian's A to Z, Vicki Adrian, 316-543-6488
Bartel Cabinet Shop, Donna or Le Wayne, 316-543-6767
Heartland Haus Antiques, 316-543-6822
LaVon's Bakery & Bar-BQ, 316-543-2411
Neufeldt's Interiors, Phil Neufeldt, 316-543-2274

BURLINGTON
1990 population 2,735
1970 population 2,099
Coffey County Chamber of Commerce, Burlington, Diana Gunlock, 316-364-2002
Coffey County Economic Development, Jon Hotaling, 316-364-8780
Beto Junction, exit 155 on I-35, 316-256-6326
Coffey County Museum, Chloe Woods, 316-364-2653
Country Critters, 316-364-8623

John Redmond Lake and Dam, 316-364-8614
Longhorn Steakhouse, 316-364-2012
Wolf Creek Tours, 316-364-4143
Wolf Creek Nature Trails, 316-364-4141

CALDWELL
1990 population 1,351
1970 population 1,540
Caldwell Chamber of Commerce, LuAnn Jamison, 316-845-6660 or 316-845-6444
Caldwell Information, Karen Sturm, 316-845-2145, or Francis Kloefkorn, 316-845-6694,
Caldwell Messenger, Damon Webber, 316-845-2320
Charles Phillips, Wilderness Photography, 316-845-2991
Chisholm Trail Information, Dave Williams, 316-845-2928
Eddie Morrison Studio, 316-845-2259
Last Chance Bar and Grill, 316-845-2434

CHERRYVALE
1990 population 2,464
1970 population 2,609
Cherryvale Chamber of Commerce, Todd Johnson, 316-336-2105
Cherryvale Chronicle, Andy Taylor, 316-336-2100
Cherryvale Information, Toddy Hosfelt, 316-336-2426
Cherryvale Museum, Fern Morrow Wood, 316-336-2090

COLBY
1990 population 5,396
1970 population 4,658
Colby Convention and Visitors Bureau, Leilani Thomas, 913-462-7643
Prairie Museum of Art and History, Sue Taylor, 913-462-4590
White's Factory Outlet, Cynthia Henningsen, 913-462-7387

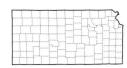

COLUMBUS
1990 population 3,268
1970 population 3,356
Columbus Chamber of Commerce, Jean Pritchett, 316-429-1492
Big Brutus, Betty Becker, 316-827-6177
Claythorne Lodge, 316-597-2568
Josie's Ristorante, 316-479-8202
Mined Land Wildlife Area, Stan Harter, 316-231-3173
Mosler Resort, 316-597-2799

CONCORDIA
1990 population 6,167
1970 population 7,221
Concordia Chamber of Commerce, Larry Blochlinger, 913-243-4290
Brown Grand Theatre, Susie Haver, 913-243-2553
Cloud County Historical Museum, 913-243-2866
Clyde Chamber of Commerce, 913-243-3300 or 913-243-3393
Crystal's Bed-and-Breakfast, 800-889-6373 or 913-243-2192
Wellspring, North Central Creative Arts, 913-243-2787

COTTONWOOD FALLS
1990 population 889
1970 population 987
Tour Kansas Guide, Jeri and Ken Harder, 316-273-8570 or 800-374-4635
Chase County Courthouse, 316-273-6493 or 316-273-8288
Cotton Wood Works, Bones Ownbey, 316-273-8274
1874 Stonehouse Bed-and-Breakfast, 316-273-8481
Emma Chase Cafe, 316-273-6020
Fiber Factory, Carol and Charley Klamm, 316-273-8686
Flint Hills Gallery, Judy Mackey, 316-273-6454
Grand Central Hotel, Suzan Barnes, 316-273-6763

Jim Bell and Son, David or Brenda Kirk, 316-273-6381
Prairie Rose Gifts, Brenda Bruch, 316-273-8151

COUNCIL GROVE
1990 population 2,228
1970 population 2,403
Council Grove Chamber of Commerce, Jola Casey, 316-767-5413
Council Grove Convention and Visitors Bureau, Jan Claves, 800-732-9211 or 316-767-5882
Council Grove Lake, Army Corps of Engineers, 316-767-5195
Cottage House Hotel-Motel, 800-727-7903 or 316-767-6828
Hays House, Rick and Alisa Paul, 316-767-5911
Kaw Mission State Historic Site, Deanne Wright, 316-767-5410

DIGHTON
1990 population 1,361
1970 population 1,540
Lane County Economic Development Alliance at Old Bank Gallery, Patrycia Herndon, 316-397-2273
Cat House Recreation, Trula or Clayton Davis, 316-397-2575
Fond Memories Antiques, Barb Newberry, 316-397-5601
Lane County Museum, Virginia Johnson, 316-397-5652

DODGE CITY
1990 population 21,129
1970 population 14,127
Dodge City Convention and Visitors Bureau, Nancy Trauer, 316-225-8186
Boot Hill Museum, Front Street, 316-227-8188
Community Event Line, 316-227-7272, ext. 8700
DCF&B Railroad, 316-225-3232
Historic information, Kansas Heritage Center, 316-227-1616
Wax Museum, 316-225-7311

DONIPHAN COUNTY
1990 population 8,134
1970 population 9,107
1890 population 13,535
Doniphan County Chamber of Commerce, Elwood, Janice Walker, 913-365-2604
Ghost Town Tours, Suzette McCord Rogers, 913-442-3304
Historical and barn tours, George N. Jorgensen, 913-985-2495
Native American Heritage Museum at Highland State Historic Site, Suzette McCord Rogers, 913-442-3304
Nelson Pharmacy, Troy, 913-985-2314
Old barn tour brochures, Courthouse, Troy, 913-985-2229
Sheila's Cafe, Troy, 913-985-3878
White Cloud information, Wolf River Bob, 913-595-3242

ELK FALLS
1990 population 122
1970 population 124
Friends of Elk Falls Association, Barry McGuire, 316-329-4433
Cape Cod Restaurant, 316-329-4379
Elk Falls Pottery Shop, 316-329-4425
Elk Falls Tannery, 316-329-4327
Elk Falls Visitor Center, 316-329-4379
Sherman House Bed-and-Breakfast, 316-329-4425

ELKHART
1990 population 2,318
1970 population 2,089
Elkhart Chamber of Commerce, Karen Brady, 316-697-4600
Cimarron National Grasslands, Joe Hartman, 316-697-4621
Dusters Baseball, Jerry Colborn, 316-697-2095
Information, Ed Johnson, 316-697-2402
Morton County Museum, 316-697-2833

ELLSWORTH
1990 population 2,294
1970 population 2,080
Ellsworth Chamber of Commerce, Charles
Jenney, 913-472-4071
Drovers Mercantile, Jim Gray or Linda Kohls,
913-472-4703
Ellsworth Museum, 913-472-3059
Fort Harker Museum, 913-472-5733
Garden Inn, Best Western Motel, 800-234-
4240 or 913-472-3116
Kanopolis Lake Legacy Trail, U.S. Corps of
Engineers at Kanopolis Lake, 913-546-
2294
Kansas Originals Market, rural Wilson, 913-
658-2602
Legacy Trail information, Jim Gray, 913-472-
4703
Wilson Chamber of Commerce, 913-658-
2211

EMPORIA
1990 population 25,512
1970 population 23,327
Emporia Convention and Visitors Bureau,
Jean-Ellen Jantzen, 800-279-3730 or 316-
342-1803
Emporia Gazette and White Memorial Park,
316-342-4800
Emporia Zoo, 316-343-4265
Lyon County Historical Museum, 316-342-
0933
National Teachers Hall of Fame, 316-341-
5660
Z Bar/Spring Hill Ranch, Barbra Zurhellen,
316-273-8494

FORT SCOTT
1990 population 8,362
1970 population 8,967
Fort Scott Chamber of Commerce, Millie
Myers-Lipscomb, 800-245-FORT or 316-
223-3566
Corner of Time, Historic Preservation Association, Kathryn Reed, 316-223-1550
Country Cupboard, Judy Renard, 316-223-

5980
Dolly the Trolley, 316-223-3678
Fort Scott National Historic Site, 316-223-
0310
The Lyons House, Pat Lyons, 316-223-0779

FREDONIA
1990 population 2,599
1970 population 3,080
Fredonia Chamber of Commerce, Gold Dust
Hotel, Carolin Ward, 316-378-3221.
Rocky Ridge Resort and Restaurant, Jack and
Mary Jo Linn, 316-378-3303
Elkhorn Sporting Clays, 316-378-2306
Friends Bird Farm and Antiques, 316-378-
3946
Stone House Gallery, 316-378-2052
Wilson County Museum, 316-378-3965

HARPER COUNTY
1990 population 7,124
1970 population 7,871
1890 population 13,266
Sunflower R.C.& D., Harper, Roger Masen-
thin, 316-896-7378.
Freeport Post Office, Carol Peterson, 316-
962-5212
Harper County Economic Development Asso-
ciation, Dollie Mathes, 316-896-2490
Harper County Historical Museum, Harper,
Gail Bellar, 316-896-2304
Restaurants, bus groups, Nelson's Restaurant,
Anthony, 316-842-5225
Runnymede Church, Gail Bellar, 316-896-
2304

HIAWATHA
1990 population 3,603
1970 population 3,365
Rural Development Association of Northeast
Kansas, Courtney Riley, Sabetha, 913-284-
3099
Hiawatha Chamber of Commerce, 913-742-
7136
Ag Museum, 913-742-6366
Brown County Historical Museum, Hiawatha,

913-742-3330
Hiawatha Heartland Inn and Resaurant, 913-
742-7401

HILLSBORO
1990 population 2,704
1970 population 2,730
Hillsboro Chamber of Commerce, Marsha
Setzkorn-Meyer, 316-947-3506
Hillsboro Arts and Crafts Fair, 316-947-3506
Irv Schroeder County Motors, 316-947-3117
Old Towne Restaurant, 316-947-5446
Pioneer Adobe House, David Wiebe, 316-947-
3775 or 316-947-3506

INMAN
1990 population 1035
1970 population 836
Community Development Coordinator, for the
City of Inman, Patricia Pries, 316-585-
2626
Inman Chamber of Commerce, Rosetta Bartels, 316-585-2166
Inman McCormick Deering Days Museum,
316-585-2626
Kansas Sampler Foundation, Marci Penner,
316-585-2374
Sounds of Kansas, Mil Penner, 316-585-2389

JEFFERSON COUNTY
1990 population 15,905
1970 population 11,945
1890 population 16,620
The Barn Bed-and-Breakfast Inn and Jeffer-
son County information, rural Valley Falls,
Tom and Marcella Ryan, 913-945-3225
Apple Valley Farm, rural Ozawkie, Meredith
Day, 913-876-2114
Frank's Pharmacy, Valley Falls, 913-945-3711
Perry Lake Project office, 913-597-5144
Snickerdoodle's Tea Room, Oskaloosa, Carole
Hendrix, 913-863-3222

KINGMAN
1990 population 3,196
1970 population 3,622

Kingman County Economic Development, Elizabeth Madden, 316-532-3694

Byron Walker Wildlife Area, Troy Smith, 316-532-3242

Cunningham information, Betty Amick, 316-298-4453

Kingman information, Lonny Bauer, 316-532-2611 or 316-532-3582

The Lumber Yard, Zenda, 316-243-6000

Zenda information, Kathleen Whitmer, 316-243-5234

LINCOLN
1990 population 1,381
1970 population 1,582

Village Lines, Marilyn Helmer, 913-524-5133

Woody House Bed-and-Breakfast, Ivona and Michael Pickering, 913-524-4744

Denmark information, Mary L. Andersen, 913-277-3685 or Mary H. Andersen, 913-526-7467

Kansas Originals Market, Marge Lawson, 913-658-2602

Spillman Creek Lodge, rural Denmark, Merrill and Kathy Nielsen, 913-277-3424

Vonada Stone Company, Duane, Donna, Damon, and Janet, rural Sylvan Grove, 913-526-7391

LINDSBORG
1990 population 3,076
1970 population 2,764

Lindsborg Chamber of Commerce, Dorene Anderson, 913-227-3706

Birger Sandzen Memorial Gallery, 913-227-2220

Brunswick Hotel and Restaurant, 913-227-2903

Malm's Smoky Valley RV Resort, 913-227-2932

Messiah Festival, 913-227-3311

Old Mill Museum, 913-227-3595

Swedish Country Inn, 913-227-2985

Swedish Crown Restaurant, 913-227-2076

LINN COUNTY
1990 population 8,254
1970 population 8,234
1890 population 17,215

Linn County Economic Development, Dennis Arnold, Mound City, 913-795-2274

Linn County Museum, Pleasanton, 913-352-8739

Lodging, Cedar Crest, Harold and Mary Jo Leisure, 913-352-6706

Marais des Cygnes Wildlife Refuge, Karl Karrow, 913-352-8941

Philippine Duchesne Shrine, Robert White, 913-649-8200

Trading Post Museum, Trading Post, 913-352-6441

LYONS
1990 population 3,688
1970 population 4,355

Rice County Economic Development Corporation, Lyons, Shirley Fair, 316-257-5166

Coronado-Quivira Museum, 316-257-3941

Hollinger's Antiques, 800-536-3711 or 316-257-3771

Prairie Flower Crafts, Alden, Sara Fair Sleeper, 316-534-3551

Santa Fe Trail information, Ralph Hathaway, 316-938-2504

McPHERSON
1990 population 12,422
1970 population 10,851

McPherson Convention and Visitors Bureau, 316-241-3340 or 800-324-8022

McPherson Chamber of Commerce, 316-241-3303

McPherson Museum, Shirley Ade, 316-245-2574

McPherson Opera House Preservation Company, 316-241-1952

McPherson Scottish Society, 800-324-8022

Main Street Deli, 316-241-1888

Belli Brothers Music Services, 316-241-5557

The Cook's Nook, 316-241-7180

MARION
1990 population 1,906
1970 population 2,052

Marion Chamber of Commerce, 316-382-3425

The Copper Shed, Ern Hett, rural Marion, 316-382-2041

Country Dreams Bed-and-Breakfast, rural Marion, Kent and Alice Richmond, 316-382-2250

Flint Hills Clay Works, 316-382-3620

Kingfisher Inn, Marion County Lake, 316-382-3755

Marion information: Diane Branson, 316-382-3165

Marion Reservoir, U.S. Army Engineer Office, 316-382-2101

Marion Historical Museum, 316-382-3432 or 316-382-2287

Trace of Copper, 316-382-2099

MAXWELL WILDLIFE REFUGE
population 200 buffalo and 75 elk

Maxwell information, 316-628-4455

MEADE
1990 population 1,526
1970 population 1,899

Dalton Gang Hideout, Nancy Dye, 800-354-2743 or 316-873-2731

Information, Nancy Ohnick at Backroom Printing, 316-873-2900 or LeRoy Lemaster, Mayor, 316-873-2224

Meade Chamber of Commerce at Meade County Museum, 316-873-2359

MEDICINE LODGE
1990 population 2,453
1970 population 2,545

Medicine Lodge, Peace Treaty Pageant, Gyp Hills Trail Rides, and Kansas Championship Ranch Rodeo information at Gallery of Western Art, Kasey Kuhn, 316-886-5163

Information, Janet Miller, 316-886-5339

Information, The Busy Bee, Aggie Bore-

den, 316-886-5021
Sagebrush Gallery, Earl Kuhn, 316-886-5163
Wildflower Tour, Barber County Conservation
    District, 316-886-3721

MORLAND
1990 population 234
1970 population 300
Information, Faye Minium, Citizens State
    Bank, 913-627-3165
Cottonwood Ranch, Don Rowlison, 913-627-
    5866
Metal artist, David Brown, 913-627-5775
Paul House Bed-and-Breakfast, Frosty and
    Alice Paul, 913-627-3875

NEMAHA COUNTY
1990 population 10,446
1970 population 11,825
1890 population 19,249
Rural Development Association, Courtney
    Riley, Sabetha, 913-284-3099.
Seneca Chamber of Commerce, Bill Miller,
    913-336-2294
Albany information, Cindy Alderfer, daytime
    913-284-2693, evening 913-284-3613, or
    Paul Huffman, 913-284-3529
Fort Markley, rural Seneca, 913-336-2285
Nemaha County Historical Museum, Seneca,
    913-336-6366
Pony Express Association, Russ Sanner, 913-
    363-2779
Village Sampler, Sabetha, Maridel Wittmer,
    913-284-2327

NESS CITY
1990 population 1,724
1970 population 1,756
Ness City Chamber of Commerce, Evelyn
    Schlegel, 913-798-2413
Cranmer Woodcrafts, Brent or Bob Cranmer,
    913-798-2849
Derrick Inn, 913-798-3617
Information, Ila Fritzler, 913-798-2237, or
    Jan Gantz, 913-798-3322
Bill Sorenson, Farmland Management Ser-

vices, 913-798-3702

NEWTON
1990 population 16,700
1970 population 15,439
Newton Convention and Tourism Bureau,
    Jacque Wedel, 316-283-7555 or 800-899-
    0455
The Breadbasket, 316-283-3811
Et Cetera Shop, 316-283-9461
Hawk House Bed-and-Breakfast, 316-283-
    2045
Kauffman Museum, 316-283-1612
Old Mill Restaurant and Bar, 316-283-3510
R J's Deli, 316-284-0056
Warkentin House Museum, 316-283-3113

PEABODY
1990 population 1,349
1970 population 1,368
City Hall, 316-983-2174 or 316-983-2175
Historical information, Muriel Wolfersperger,
    316-983-2193
Jones Bed-and-Breakfast, Marilyn Jones, 316-
    983-2815
Mayesville Mercantile, Gary Jones, 316-983-
    2210
Phoenix Dry Goods, Steve Hamous, 316-983-
    2340
Sharon's Kountry Kitchen, 316-983-2307
Turkey Red Restaurant, Mike Collins, 316-
    983-2888

PITTSBURG
1991 population 17,775
1970 population 20,171
Crawford County Visitors Bureau, Robbi Pazz-
    ie, 316-231-1212, or 800-879-1112
Crawford County Historical Museum, Pitts-
    burg, 316-231-1440
Frontenac information, Ted Hauser, 316-231-
    9210
Girard Chamber of Commerce, Maxine Harris
    316-724-4715
Girard Drive-By Tours, Terry Harley, 316-724-
    4317 or 316-724-4570

Mined Land Wildlife Area, Stan Harter, 316-
    231-3173 Crawford

PRATT
1990 population 6,687
1970 population 6,736
Pratt Chamber of Commerce, Jeanette
    Siemens, 316-672-5501
The Coffee Trader, John and Michele Martin,
    316-672-7400
Kansas Department of Wildlife and Parks,
    Bob Mathews, 316-672-5911
Main Street Antique Mall, Pat Lickiss, 316-
    672-6770
Peggy's, 316-672-5648
Phil's "54" Diner, 316-672-3900
Pratt County Historical Museum, 316-672-
    7874
Simply Southwest, Terry Siroky, 316-672-
    7722

RAWLINS COUNTY
1990 population 3,404
1970 population 4,393
1890 population 6,756
Rawlins County Economic Development,
    Arlene Bliss, Atwood, 913-626-3017
McDonald Grocery Store, McDonald, Brenda
    Johnson, 913-538-2528
Ol' Depot, Atwood, 913-626-3114
Pooch's Pizza, Herndon, ask for Harold, 913-
    322-5361
Rawlins County Historical Museum, Atwood,
    Craig Cox, 913-626-3885

STOCKTON
1990 population 1,507
1970 population 1,818
City of Stockton Economic Development,
    Linda Yohon, 913-425-6162
Damar information, Country Folks Restau-
    rant, Leona Newell, 913-838-4320
Nicodemus information, Angela Bates-Tomp-
    kins, 913-674-3311 or 913-674-2084
Rooks County Museum, Stockton, 913-425-
    7217